Coastal Zones of the Pacific
A Descriptive Atlas

Pacific Circle Consortium

and

Oregon Sea Grant

ORESU-B-96-001

Sandy Ridlington, atlas coordinator and editor
Marguerite Wells, writer and researcher
Francis M. Pottenger III, project coordinator
Don Poole and Anna Asquith, artists
Tom Weeks, designer

Published by Oregon Sea Grant
Oregon State University
402 Administrative Services
Corvallis, Oregon 97331-2134

ISBN: 1-881826-06-6

Contents

Foreword

This atlas of the coastal zones of the Pacific is the work of The Ocean Project (TOP), a collaborative effort by representatives of Pacific nations to promote understanding of their shared environment, the Pacific Ocean, and to enrich learning about it.

Educators in the participating organizations believe that Pacific peoples must share in decisions about the uses of the ocean. To do this we need to understand the nature of the coastal zone, the ecosystems of the Pacific coastal zones, and the problems that threaten these ecosystems.

The premise of TOP is that a set of cross-cultural materials collaboratively developed can empower students to understand and empathize with the concerns, needs, and ways of life of other Pacific peoples.

The atlas is for students 13 to 17 years old, particularly those in English-speaking areas of the Pacific.

We are bound by the ties of friendship and common purpose, but the English speakers among us are riven by two petty and perennial disputes. We spell the English language differently and we use different systems of measurement. We have therefore come to a compromise on the grounds of both equity and science: we have chosen to use American spelling and the decimal system. That way, everybody suffers and everyone gains from a new intellectual demand.

There is an exception to this. In matters of international law, the world uses measures such as nautical miles, and we have done so too.

Preface

Why is the coastal zone important to the peoples of the Pacific? We use it in many ways and depend on its resources. Millions of people live, work, and spend their leisure time near the coast.

But it is not only human beings who thrive in the coastal zone. It provides habitats for a great diversity of living things. Most of the fish and shellfish eaten by peoples of the Pacific are caught there.

The fragile ecosystems of the coastal zone are quickly destroyed by environmental change. We human beings, often mindless agents of such change, cause pollution and erosion, mine and dredge the coastal zone, clear mangrove swamps, and drain wetlands. These activities severely affect the plant and animal life and eventually the human beings who depend on the resources in this region of land and sea. Our coastal zones are crucial environmental, economic, and aesthetic resources that are at risk. As a result, the peoples of the Pacific need to have a thorough knowledge of the ecology and economics of the coastal zone.

This atlas defines the coastal zone and describes the different kinds of coast found in and along the Pacific. It explains currents and winds as well as the ecosystems of the various kinds of coast. It details threats to the coast from pollution and ends with a discussion of how the coast can be managed.

Coastal Zones of the Pacific presents generalizations rather than specifics about coastal zones. The atlas is a resource providing information by means of maps and graphs, with a limited text highlighting the important ideas and issues associated with the coastal zone. These ideas include the concepts of conservation and sustainable yield. It is not a textbook. Students can use it to identify issues and to develop questions for further investigation. It can also be used to structure a framework for research. It is intended to stimulate thought, generate ideas, and lead students to further individual investigations.

Acknowledgments

The initiative for The Ocean Project (TOP) came from the Pacific Circle Consortium, a group of educational agencies established under the auspices of the Center for Educational Research and Innovation (CERI) of the Organization for Economic Cooperation and Development (OECD). Contributing researchers, with the organizations they represent, are

Australia:
Marguerite Wells, University of Wollongong

New Zealand:
Barry L. Stringer and Denis E. Martin,
Marlborough Boys' College, Blenheim,
New Zealand

South Pacific Commission:
Neva Wendt, South Pacific Regional Environment
Programme, Noumea, New Caledonia

United States:
Francis M. Pottenger III, Curriculum Research
and Development Group, University of Hawaii
Sandy Ridlington, Oregon Sea Grant,
Oregon State University
Vicki Osis, Extension Sea Grant,
Oregon State University

Introduction

Nobody knows the total length of all the coastlines in the world. Although the thousands of islands in the Pacific are small, they add greatly to the length of the world's coastline.

What do we mean by coastline? A coastline is obviously the line where the land meets the sea, but that line is constantly changing. The tides come in and go out. The waves wash over the beach and withdraw, and they beat higher or lower against the cliffs. Sometimes a storm or tsunami can change the outline of the coast. There are islands, such as Sakurajima, a volcanic island in southern Japan, that appeared suddenly from the sea. Other volcanic islands explode and disappear. Falcon Island near Tonga is a young active volcano that is sometimes there and sometimes not. In Napier, New Zealand, an airport is built on land that did not exist in 1930. The land rose out of the sea during an earthquake. Perhaps the most complicated coastline is that of an island with a barrier reef. Such an island, in fact, has three coastlines—the outer, where the waves break, the landward side of the reef, and the island's beach.

Many ocean animals live sometimes in the sea and sometimes on land. Seabirds fish in the ocean and come to land to nest; many kinds of plants and seaweeds grow only near the coast. Some, such as mangroves, grow in salt swamps with their roots in the sea. Coral lives near the surface of the sea, and at low tide you can walk from the land out onto a fringing reef that appears to be part of the land.

Sea creatures or the battering of waves may break down coral, forming sand that in the end washes up on the beach and becomes land. On the other hand, when rivers wash silt, rocks, and waste down to the sea, what was once part of the land becomes part of the seabed.

What Is a Coastal Zone?

How Far out to Sea?

Where is the edge of your country? If you are in a boat near the shore and you commit a crime, can the law punish you? There was a time when the ability of a nation to enforce its laws was limited by how far it could shoot. Anything out of cannon shot of the shore was beyond the reach of the law.

A lighthouse in Oregon

Until about a century ago, the legal "coastal zone" of a country was its "territorial sea," three nautical miles from shore. Within this zone, a nation was able to stop other nations from fishing.

In the twentieth century, as fishing rights became more valuable, some nations declared territorial zones of 12 nautical miles. Today all Pacific countries claim twelve nautical miles of territorial sea, except Australia and Singapore, which stop at three, and the Philippines, which claims many more.

In the 1940s, oil and gas were discovered on the continental shelves. As a result a number of nations extended their claim to 200 nautical miles. This territory developed into a 200-mile "exclusive fishing zone" (EFZ), or "exclusive economic zone" (EEZ).

In the 1980s the United Nations Convention on the Law of the Sea (UNCLOS) added the contiguous zone (24 nautical miles), in which nations had more limited legal control than in the territorial seas.

There was also, of course, the natural zone, the continental shelf. This area is the part of the continent that lies under the sea. UNCLOS legally defined the continental shelf as an area controlled by the nation that it borders.

Now over 40 percent of the oceans are claimed by some country or other. Of all the oceans in the world, the area claimed in the Pacific is greatest because of its thousands of islands. Compare the size of New Zealand's EEZ with that of Australia. The United States claims a huge zone around the Hawaiian islands, far from the continental shelf. Japan claims a circle 200 miles in radius around a rock called Minami-tori-shima (Marcus Island), nearly half way between Japan and Hawaii. The sea is wearing away this rock, and the Japanese continue to rebuild it with concrete blocks to keep it from disappearing completely.

An oil rig in Bass Strait, between the states of Victoria and Tasmania

How Far onto the Land?

As people began to travel the world and sail in the waters of other nations, they began to see a need for international law. One of the most important problems in international law has been to define how far out to sea the coastal zone goes. The next question is how far it extends onto the land. This question is for a country's own lawmakers to decide.

In the 1970s, people had just started using the words "pollution" and "conservation." Many in the world had begun to realize that the environment was threatened and that we need to conserve the rich resources of coastal zones for future generations. At the same time, because these resources are so rich, other people saw the coastal zone as a good place to build, mine, reclaim land, and do those things called "development."

Throughout the world, laws were passed controlling the use of the coastal zone. One of the earliest sets of laws was passed in the United States. It defined the zone as "coastal waters and adjacent shorelands strongly influenced by each other." This set of laws stated that the coastal zone extended inland as far as was needed to allow control over human uses that would have a direct effect on coastal waters.

For the atlas, we have adapted this early definition.

Throughout the book, "coastal zone" refers to the part of the land that strongly influences the sea, and the part of the sea that strongly influences the land.

What's Special about the Coastal Zone?

Of all ocean habitats, mangroves produce the most life. Coral reefs are next and then estuaries, lagoons, and continental shelves. Although the coastal zone is narrow, almost all of the living things of the ocean begin their lives there. Where there is no food, fish and other sea creatures cannot live. The life of the ocean depends on the amount of plankton and sea plants it can produce. Almost all of the food is produced in the coastal zone. Whereas the open ocean is a desert, the coastal zone is a rich, lush garden, seething with life.

Why is the open ocean a desert? In the open sea, the phytoplankton live in the top layers of the water, where there is light. In the summer, a layer of warm water lies on top of colder water, which grows even colder the deeper it is. Underneath these layers is the huge mass of ocean water that never warms up at all. Hardly any water moves from one layer to another. There is almost no circulation while the top layers remain warm. As the living things of the top layer die, they sink, and so the top layer

loses nutrients quickly. However, in the autumn and winter,
as the top layer cools down and
storms break up the layers of
water, there is much more
circulation and nutrients start
to rise to the surface. During
this time, the productivity of
the deep ocean increases, but it
is always lower than that of the
coastal zone.

In the coastal zone the story
is different. Nutrients wash
down from the land. Layers do
not form in the shallower,
warmer waters of this zone,
and so the nutrients circulate
more freely than in the open
ocean. Where there is a lot of
food, living things can thrive.
That is why the coastal zone
teems with life.

*The Shrinking High Seas. Over 40
percentof the world's oceans are claimed
by some country or other. This map
shows some—but not all—of the ocean
area claimed by Pacific countries as
exclusive economic zones.*

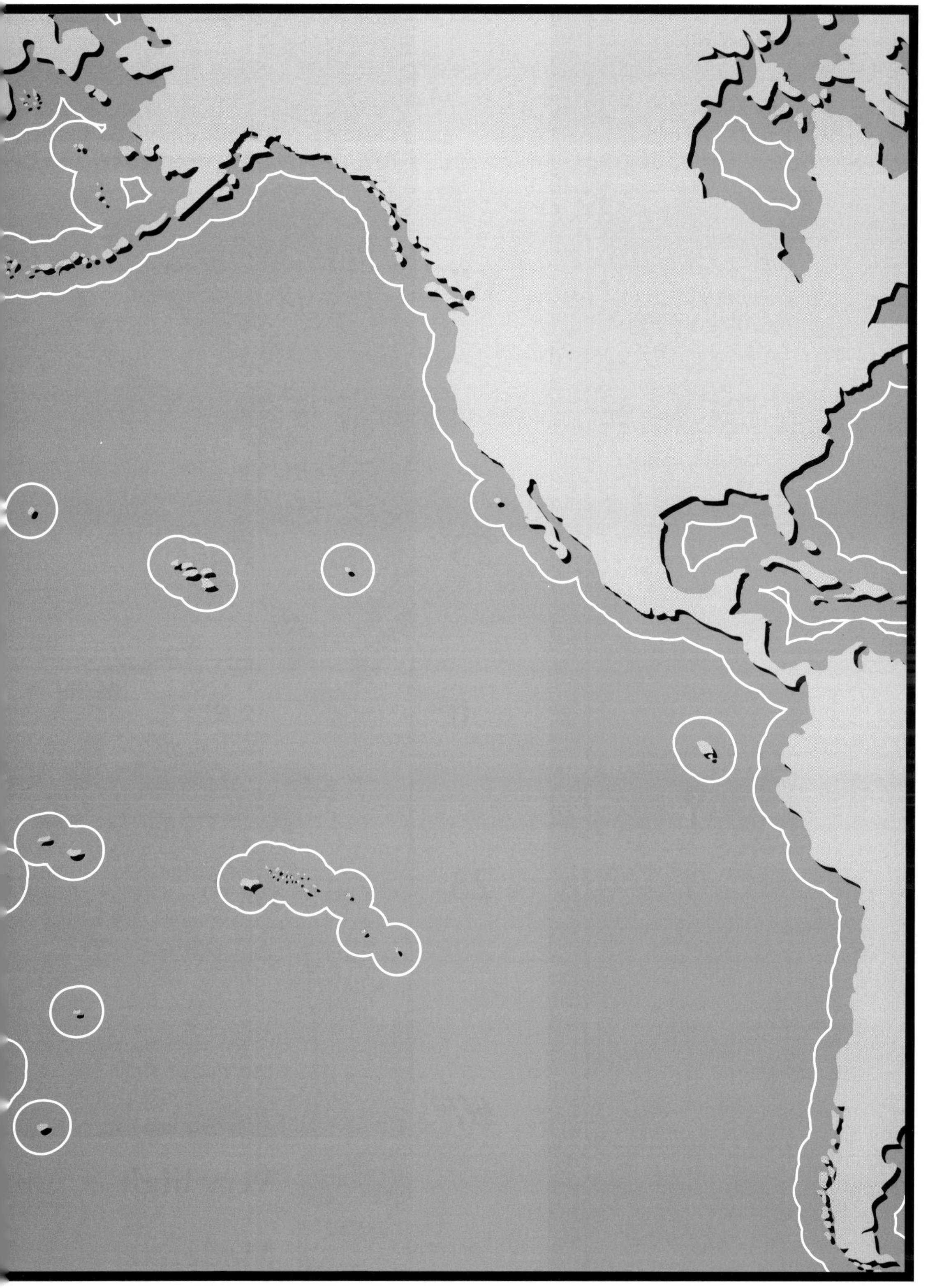

*High-productivity regions of the
Pacific Ocean*

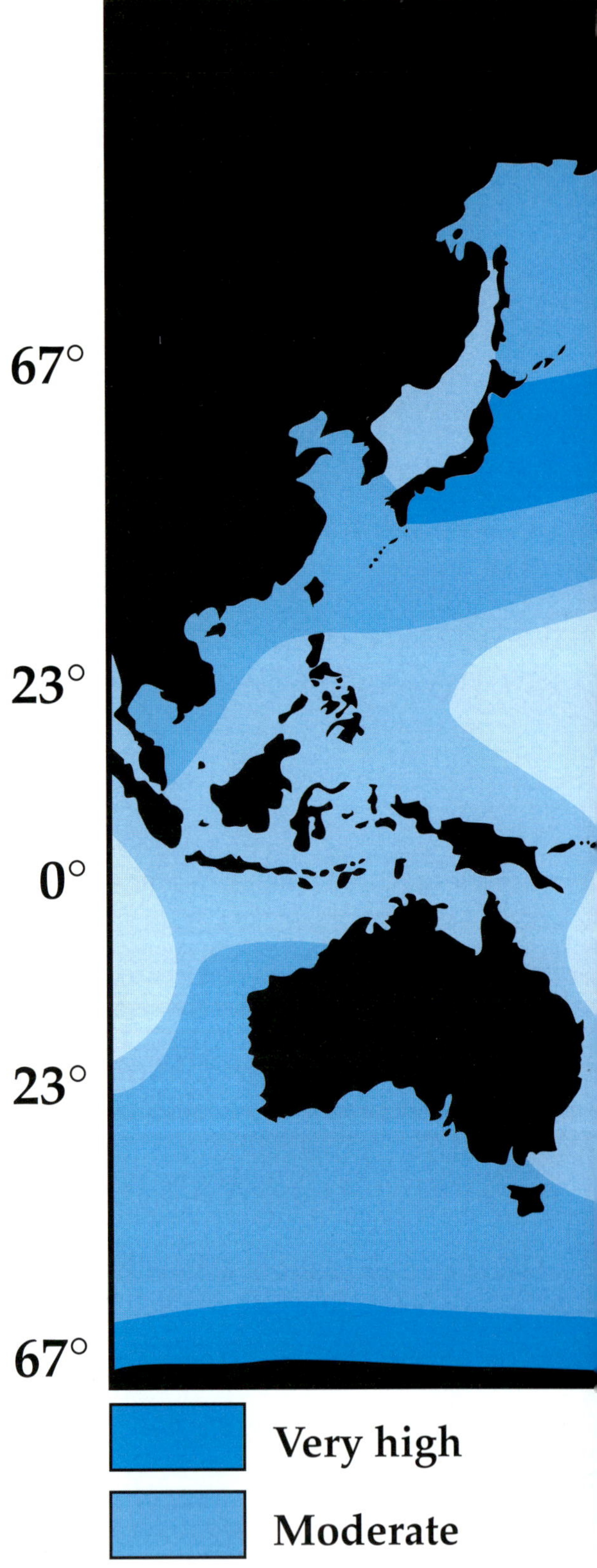

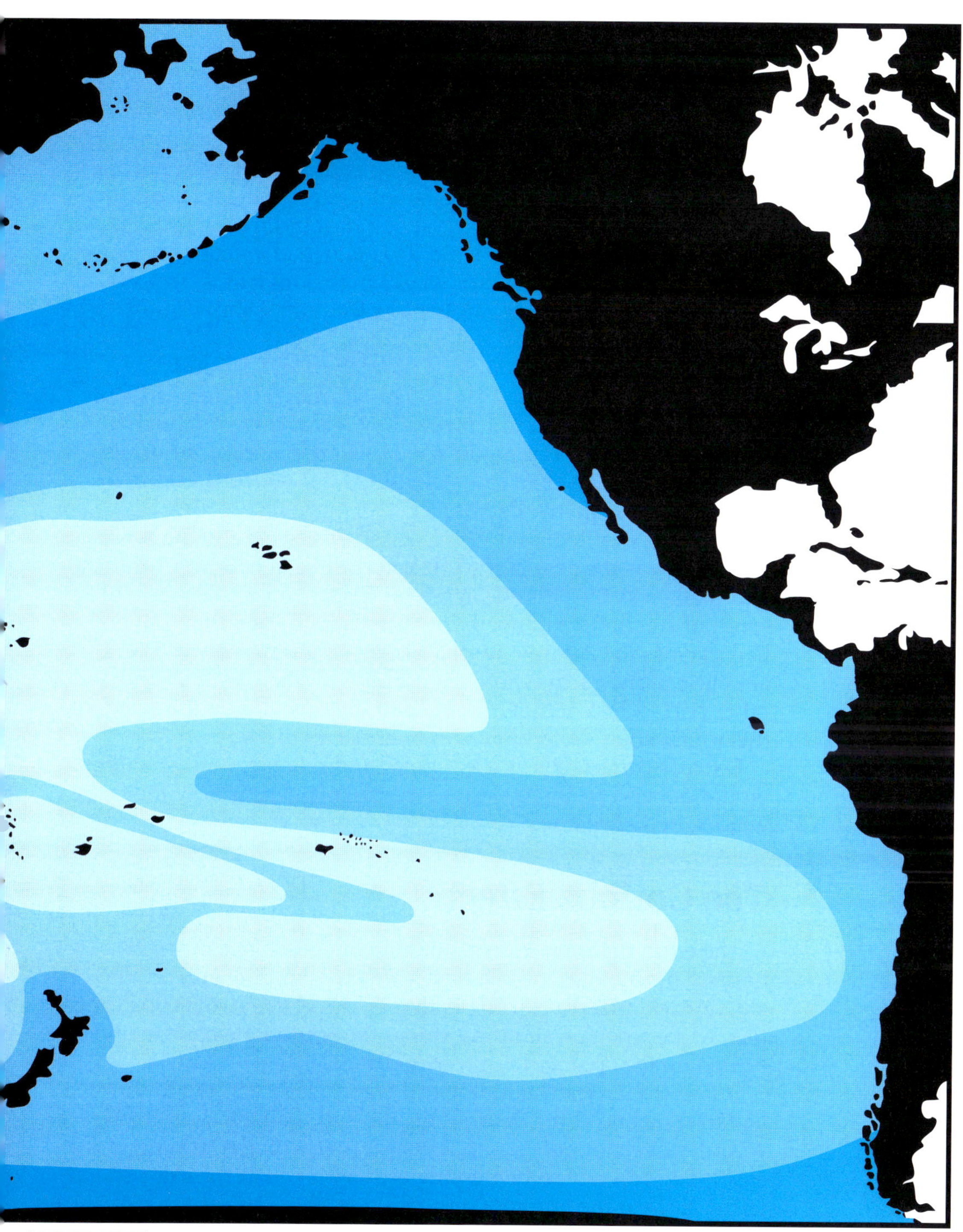

Low
Very low to nil

Winds and Currents

In the days of sailing ships, you could travel from Europe to the Pacific by three different routes. You could follow the coast of Africa, and then go past India and through Indonesia into the Pacific. This way had a major problem: you could get stuck for weeks in the doldrums, regions of the earth where the wind rarely blows; a sailing ship cannot move without wind.

You could cross the Atlantic, follow the coast of South America, and round Cape Horn. This journey was very difficult because where the Atlantic meets the Pacific, there are huge waves and storms. You might have to wait in harbor for weeks for a good day and then lose your ship, and yourself, trying to break through into the Pacific.

The third way looks silly, but, if you were going to the South Pacific, it was the best of the lot. You could sail to South America and then cross the Atlantic again to Africa. You could then sail south of Australia and north into the Pacific. Even though you had to cross the Atlantic twice, this was the fastest way. There are parts of the earth where the wind blows hardly at all and other parts where it blows almost all the time. If you followed this route, you would have wind almost all the way.

Because certain winds are regular and reliable, trading ships would depend on them to cross the oceans. This is how the trade winds got their name.

The Coriolis Effect

The earth turns on its axis, making one full circle every 24 hours. This means that in a day, someone standing still on the equator will make a full circle, that is, travel about 40,000 kilometers, while a person standing still at the South Pole has merely turned on the spot and not traveled at all.

If you stood on the equator and were strong enough to throw a ball to someone at the South Pole, the ball, as it left your hand, would move, not only south, but also east with the turning of the earth. The ball would be moving east with you at the same speed as the earth at the moment you threw it. Therefore as the ball traveled south it would bend to the east. At about one-third of the way to the pole it would move almost due east and would thus not reach the South Pole at all.

For the same reason, a ball thrown from the North Pole would lag well behind the turning of the earth as it moved toward the equator.

This influence on moving bodies, called the Coriolis effect, affects winds and ocean currents as well as balls.

The Coriolus effect

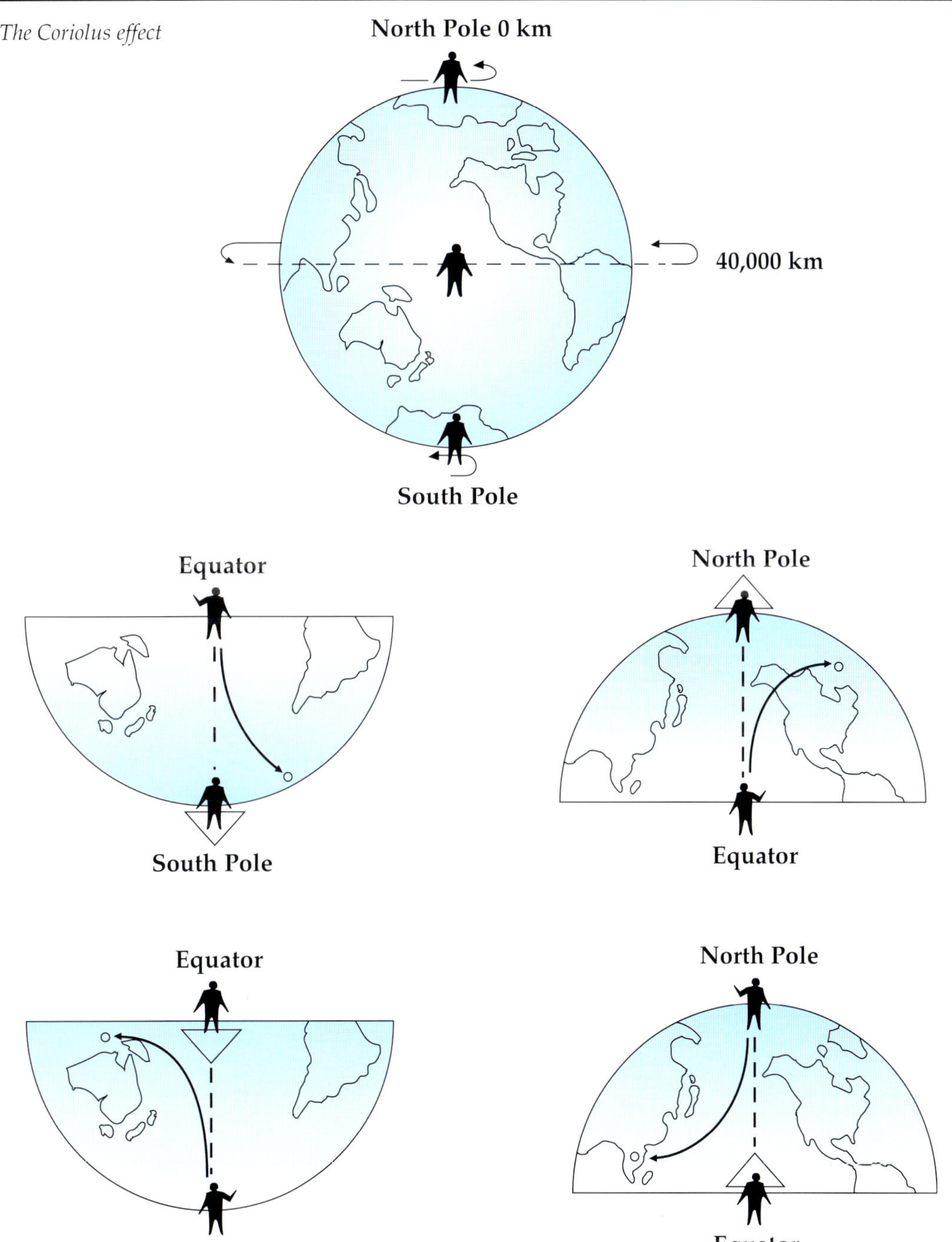

Winds

Imagine that the earth is all water. The equator is the line encircling the earth half way between the poles. Its nights and days are of equal length, and its temperature is always hot. A great deal of water evaporates there, and hot, moist air will rise. Cooler air from the north and south is drawn toward the equator over the surface of the ocean, creating a circulation of air.

Because of the Coriolis effect, circulating air comes at sea level toward the equator from the east. These air currents are the trade winds.

Where the hot air rises at the equator, there will not be much wind. It is here that sailing ships used to float for weeks without a breath of air to fill their sails. These areas are the doldrums.

Of course the whole system is much more complicated than this. For a start, the earth is not completely covered by water. Land heats and cools faster than seawater. This means that the air above the land and the air above the sea are at different temperatures, rising and sinking at different times and different speeds and thus causing variable winds.

Upwellings

The nutrients of the ocean (minerals from the land and detritus from the bodies of living things) sink to the ocean floor. In some places they can be brought to the surface by upwelling. Winds blowing from the land to the sea continually move surface waters away from the coast and bring to the surface cold water rich in the nutrients that have been

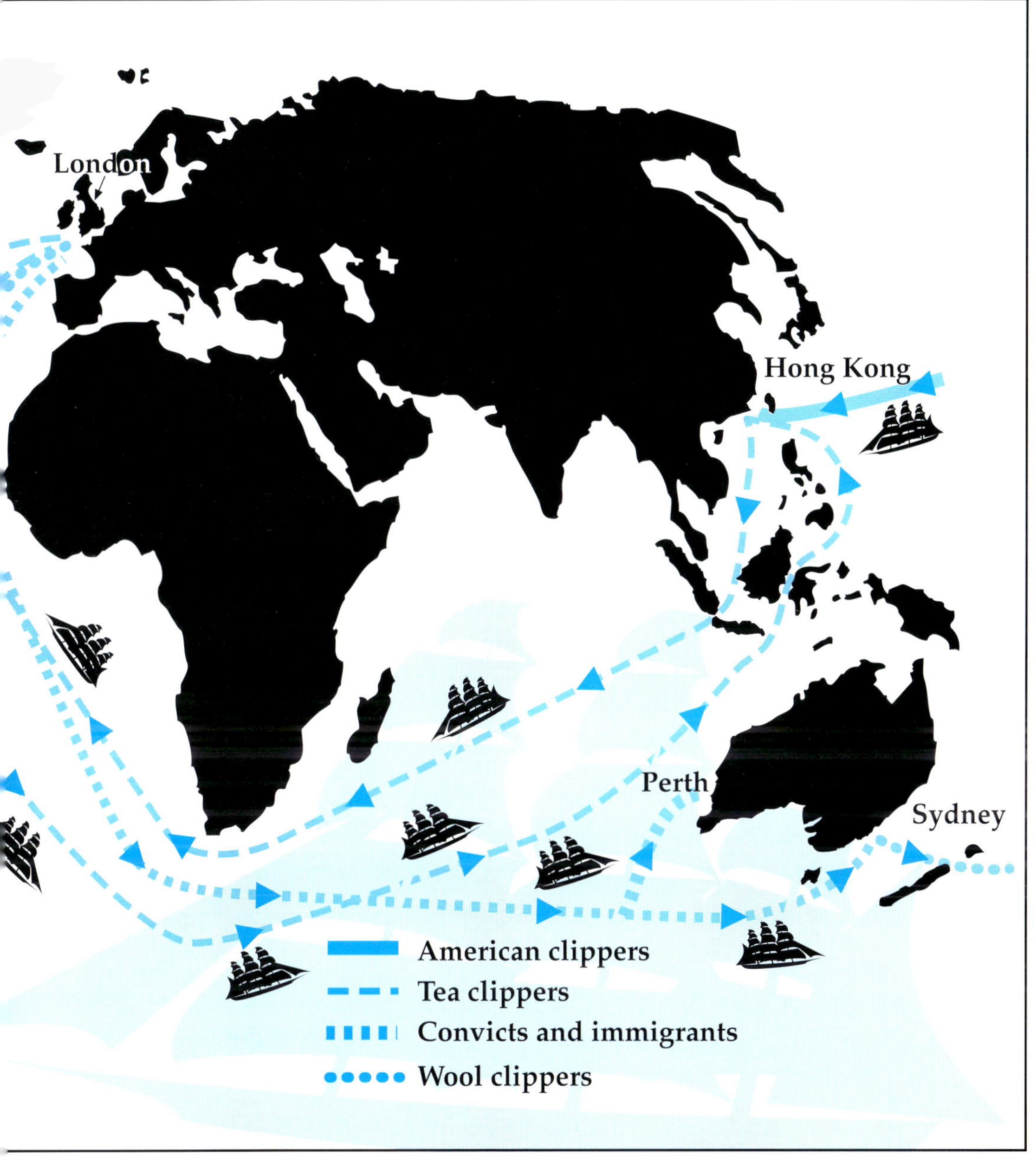

building up in the depths. Therefore, where there is an upwelling there is also a rich fishing ground. In the Pacific extensive areas of upwellings are found near Peru and Oregon; there are also many small ones in coastal areas throughout the Pacific.

Because seabirds feed on fish, land near upwellings draws large bird populations. They leave their droppings on coastal shores and islands. The droppings, known as guano,

Routes of the early traders. Trading ships depended on regular, reliable winds.

are rich in phosphates and nitrates, excellent foods for plants. The island of Nauru, made almost entirely of guano, mines guano for fertilizer. Feeding the gardens of the world, the Nauruan people have become among the richest people in the world, but their island is now a wasteland.

The land near an upwelling can be coastal desert because if there is to be an upwelling, winds must blow from the land to the sea, carrying away moisture from the land.

Currents

The winds whip up waves, resulting in a slow movement of the surface waters. These relentlessly moving waters are ocean currents. If you look at the map of the currents of the Pacific, you can see that they follow the pattern of the winds.

The waters near the equator are warm and those near the poles are cold, so the currents may carry warm water into cold areas and cold water into warm areas of the world. This means, for example, that southern Japan, where you would expect the ocean to be cold, is warmed by a current from the equator and so has coral.

Because land lying in the path of cold currents is cooled, islands near the equator that could be expected to have a very hot climate and coral may instead have a mild climate and no coral. For example, the Galapagos Islands on the equator near South America have penguins and fur seals that you would expect to find on the southernmost coasts of Australia and New Zealand. The Marquesas, which are also in the path of a cold current, have little coral, even though they are well within the tropics.

Currents may also carry nutrient-rich waters from one place to another. Where these waters come to the surface, causing a rapid growth of plankton, productive fishing grounds may be found. This happens up the Pacific coast of South America where the cold, nutrient-rich Antarctic waters are carried by the Humboldt current north towards the Galapagos Islands, producing rich fishing grounds off the coast of Chile.

Local currents may be produced by tides or by the outflow from rivers.

Effects of a land mass on ocean winds. This coastal range helps convert moist ocean air to drier air that moves inland.

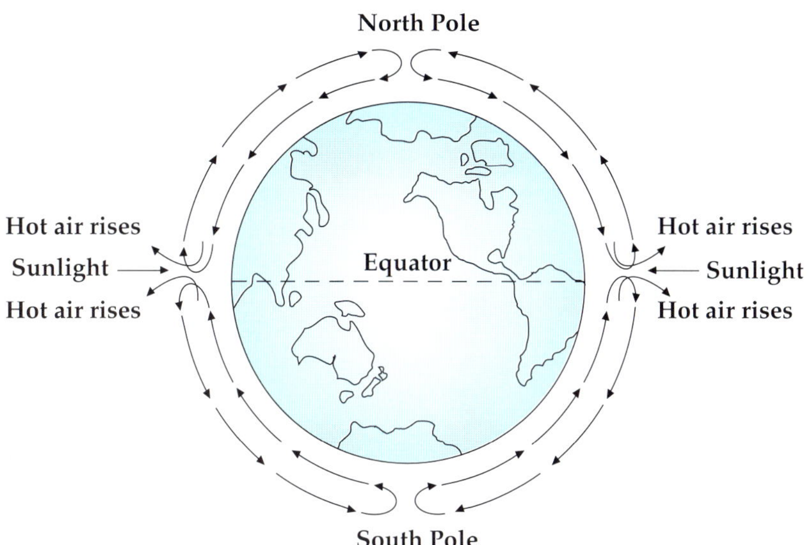

Circulation of the atmosphere

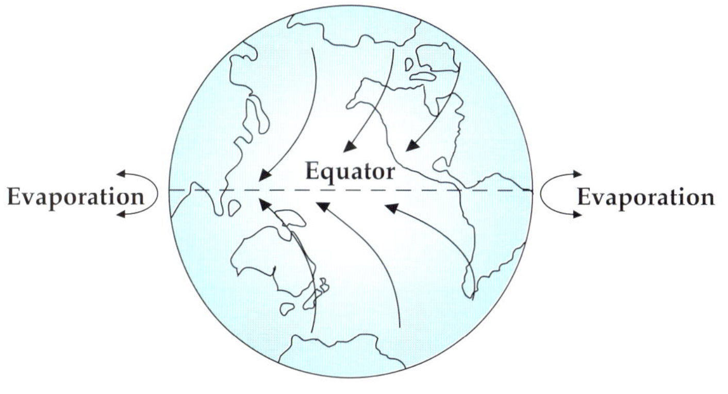

Results of the Coriolus effect

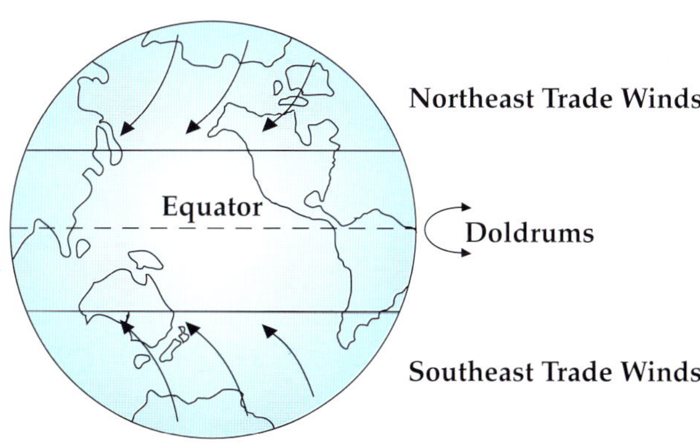

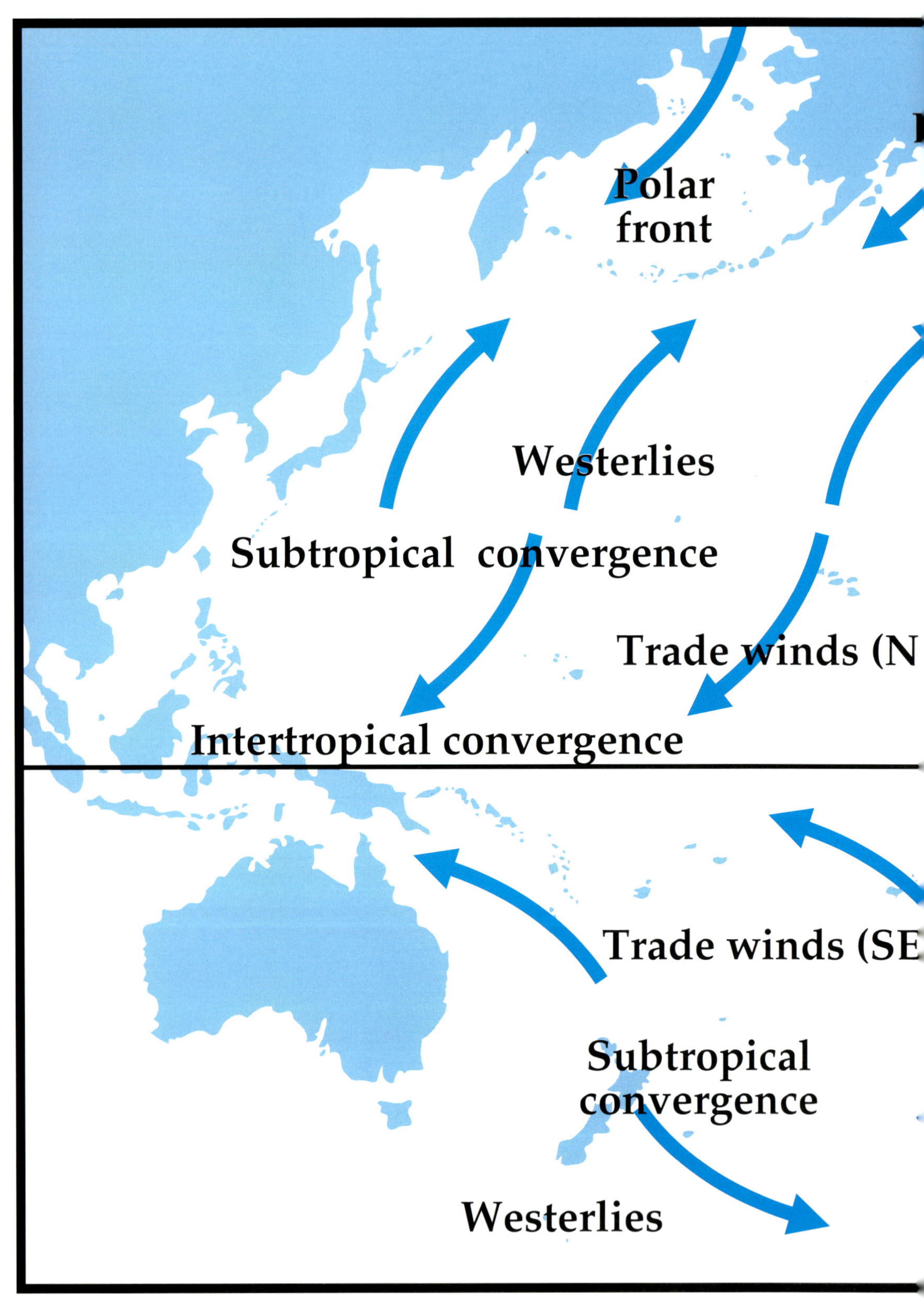

Polar
front
Westerlies
Subtropical convergence
Trade winds (N
Intertropical convergence
Trade winds (SE
Subtropical
convergence
Westerlies

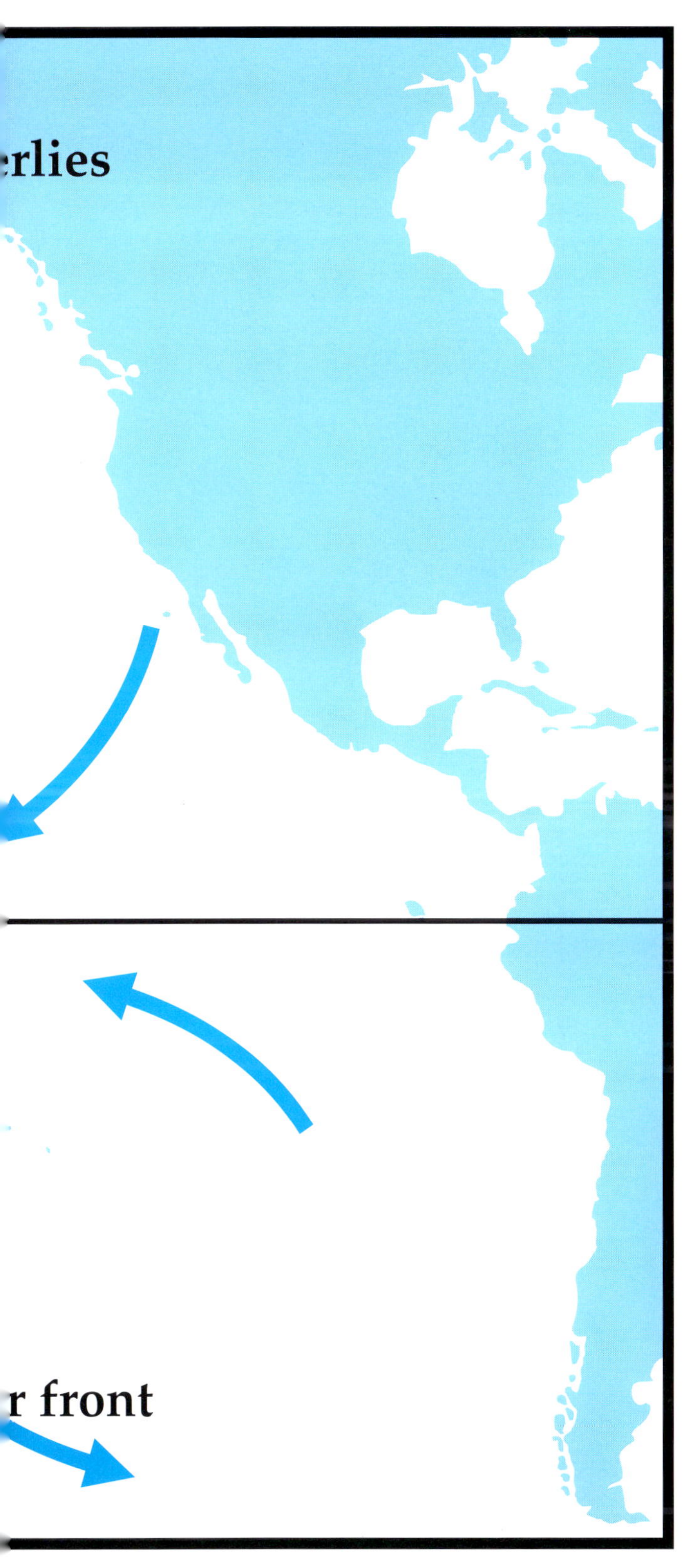

Patterns of surface winds in the Pacific

Patterns of surface currents in the Pacific

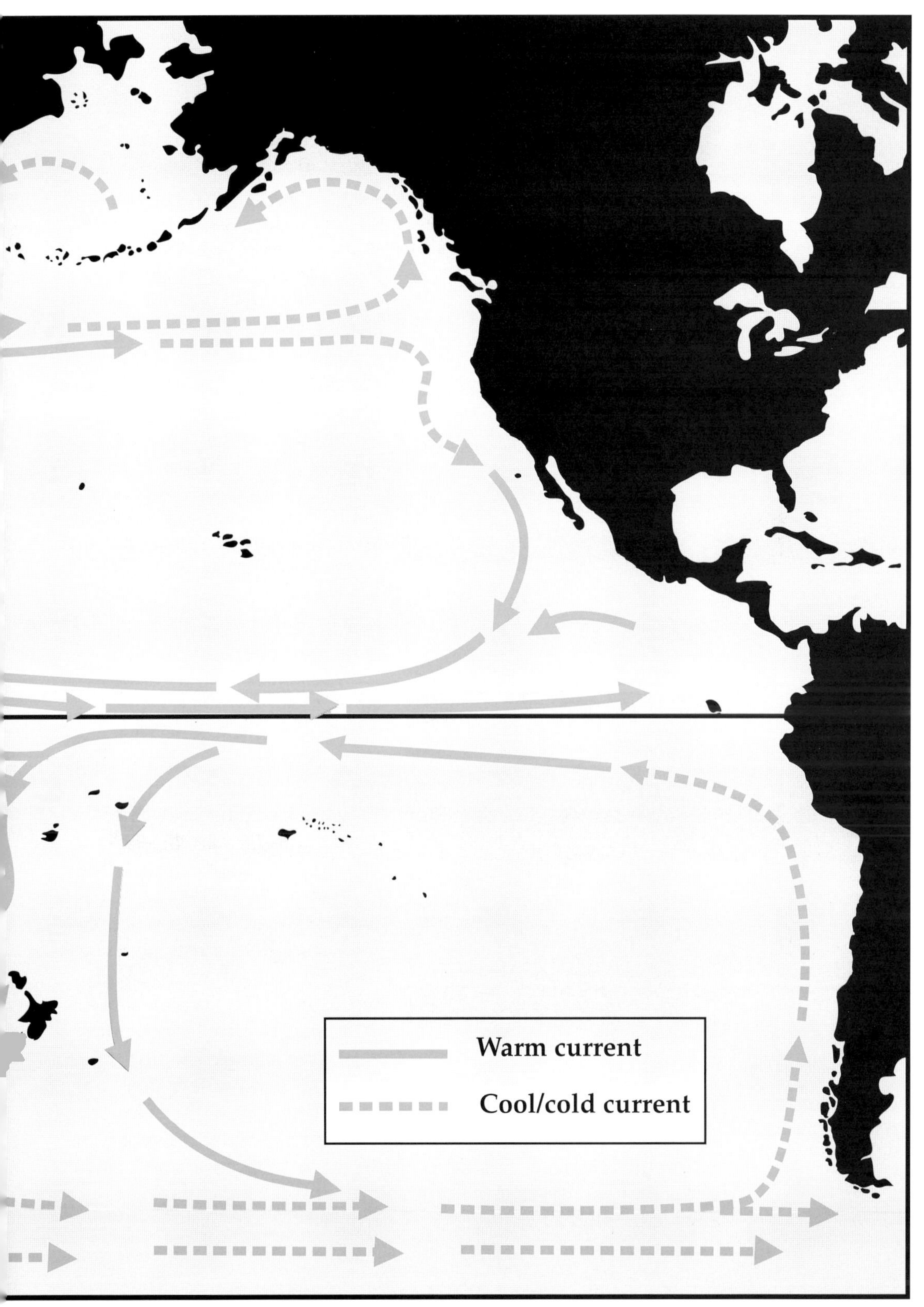

Warm current
Cool/cold current

Beaches and Cliffs

When we think of a beach, we tend to think of white sand, but there are many other types of beach: rocky beaches, gravel beaches, black, and even red sand beaches. We can think of a beach as a buffer zone that protects the land from the attack of the waves.

Beach material is not there by chance. Either the waves have carried it onto the beach or it has fallen onto the beach from the land above.

When a wave breaks on a steeply sloping beach, it loses energy suddenly, dropping the pebbles and sand that it carries. Then the fine sand is swept up in the strong backwash out to sea, leaving behind only the rocks. In this way a rocky beach is formed or maintained.

Waves reaching a gentle slope lose their energy gradually. Heavier particles drop first, then the lighter ones. By the time waves reach the shore, they are carrying only fine sand. Sand already on the beach stays there because there is no strong backwash to carry it away. There may be rocks underneath, but you can't see them because they are covered with sand. Thus, a sandy beach is created by the lapping of waves on a gently sloping shore.

Some beaches are formed of materials that erode from cliffs. Oregon, USA.

The land slopes most steeply down to the sea where there are cliffs. Waves break directly against the cliffs, eating them away. The backwash from this violent action carries away most of the sediment. Thus, sand does not build up around cliffs and headlands. Instead, caves and arches form, and if they collapse, they leave only piles of rocks.

Sand and gravel are also composed of shells, bits of coral and algae, and the skeletons of sponges, crabs, and shrimp. Bones and shells, composed of calcium carbonate, usually form white sands that may be compressed and turned into limestone.

When quartz rock breaks down, it produces another white sand; basalt produces black sand. Some beaches in the South Pacific are made of ground-up, red, pipe-organ coral. Others are made of green, volcanic olivine. Some beaches on the west coast of New Zealand are black sand, which is iron oxide. These sands are mined to produce iron ore.

A boulder beach on a moderately exposed shore. The strong waves carry the sand out to sea, leaving the boulders behind. Nelson, South Island, New Zealand.

An almost flat beach. Waves lap gently, carrying in small particles and forming a wide beach of fine sand. Tugun Beach, Australia.

The gentle slope of the beach in the cove has accumulated sand. The cliffs have not. Loch Ard Gorge, Victoria, Australia.

Living with Tides

Everything that makes its home within reach of the tide must be able to live sometimes in seawater and sometimes in air. When the tide is in, the world of the shore is cool, wet, and dim. When the tide is out in the daytime, the shore is dry, the sun blazes down, and the animals are inactive. They need to stay moist in order to breathe, and they need to keep cool. They can remain moist or cool by crawling back into the water, by staying in the spray zone, by sealing themselves up, by staying in the shade, or by burrowing. If the tide is out at night the animals or plants may face different problems, such as low temperatures.

Violent wave action forms arches. In January 1991, this formation collapsed. London Bridge, Victoria, Australia.

Living with Variety

Conditions are not the same on all parts of the shore. At the high-water mark, plants and animals live in air for most of their lives. At the low-water mark, they are exposed to air for only a few minutes, twice each day, when the tide is fully out. Most plants and animals can live successfully within only a limited range, and most of them therefore live in specific zones on the shore.

Where the range of tides is small and the beach is steep, the zones are narrow. Where the tidal range is great and the slope is flat, the zones are wide. Zones depend on many factors, such as changes in temperature, salinity, and wave action, and since these factors change, the zones can change too. Animals and plants must find a home for themselves in the zone to which they are adapted. If they do not, they will die. On the upper parts of the shore, most of the living things are animals. Seaweeds tend to live farther down.

Some plants and animals are not found in well-defined zones. They may live under stones, in rock pools, under seaweeds or overhangs, in crevices, or in surge channels where conditions will be quite different from those on exposed rocks.

Different plants and animals live at different levels above the water-line, forming zones of various shades.

Sandy Beaches

Because sand constantly shifts with the movement of water, sandy beaches are not hospitable to plants. Plants need to send their roots down into firm earth and thus do not put down roots on such beaches. And seaweeds, which do not have roots, find it difficult to anchor because of the constant movement of the sand. Animals that build a permanent home also find it difficult to live on sandy beaches. If they try to dig a burrow, the sand falls in on them or is washed away by the next tide. Thus, animals living beneath the sand have to repair their burrows constantly or else imbed themselves again.

Life fares better on gently sloping beaches protected from wave action. Fine particles of organic matter can be deposited there. Also, microscopic plants can live beneath the surface of the sand. This means that more food and therefore more animals are found on beaches having a gradual slope.

Like the plants and animals on rocky shores, those of the sandy beach live in zones. Living things that require more seawater are closer to the ocean, and those that need a drier lifestyle live higher up the shore.

Rocky Shores

When the waves are beating against the shore, the animals and plants need to be strong enough to cling to the rock so that they do not get washed out to sea or carried higher onto the beach where they will dry out. Living on a rocky shore is hazardous. Organisms are in danger of being injured by the waves, being carried away by them, drying out, changing temperature, or being eaten.

Human beings are a problem too. They send sewage and pollution from chemical wastes onto the beach, and this may kill the animals and plants. As tourists they trample the shores or collect animals, which then die.

Rock Pools

As the tide goes out it leaves pools of seawater among the rocks. Plants and animals living in the pools face many problems. They have to be able to live with high temperatures and low oxygen levels. No new seawater comes in until high tide. In rock pools, warmed by the sun and chilled by night winds, it is both hotter during the day and colder at night than in the sea. Plants provide shade and give off oxygen, and animals breathe in oxygen. In some rock pools, though, there are no plants, and animals living there may have a shortage of oxygen. The saltiness of the water, the amount of light, and the buildup of waste products may also make it harder for things to live in a rock pool.

Seaweeds living on rocky shores need to be able to withstand the force of the waves. They are often firmly attached to rocks by holdfasts, and their bodies may be strong and leathery.

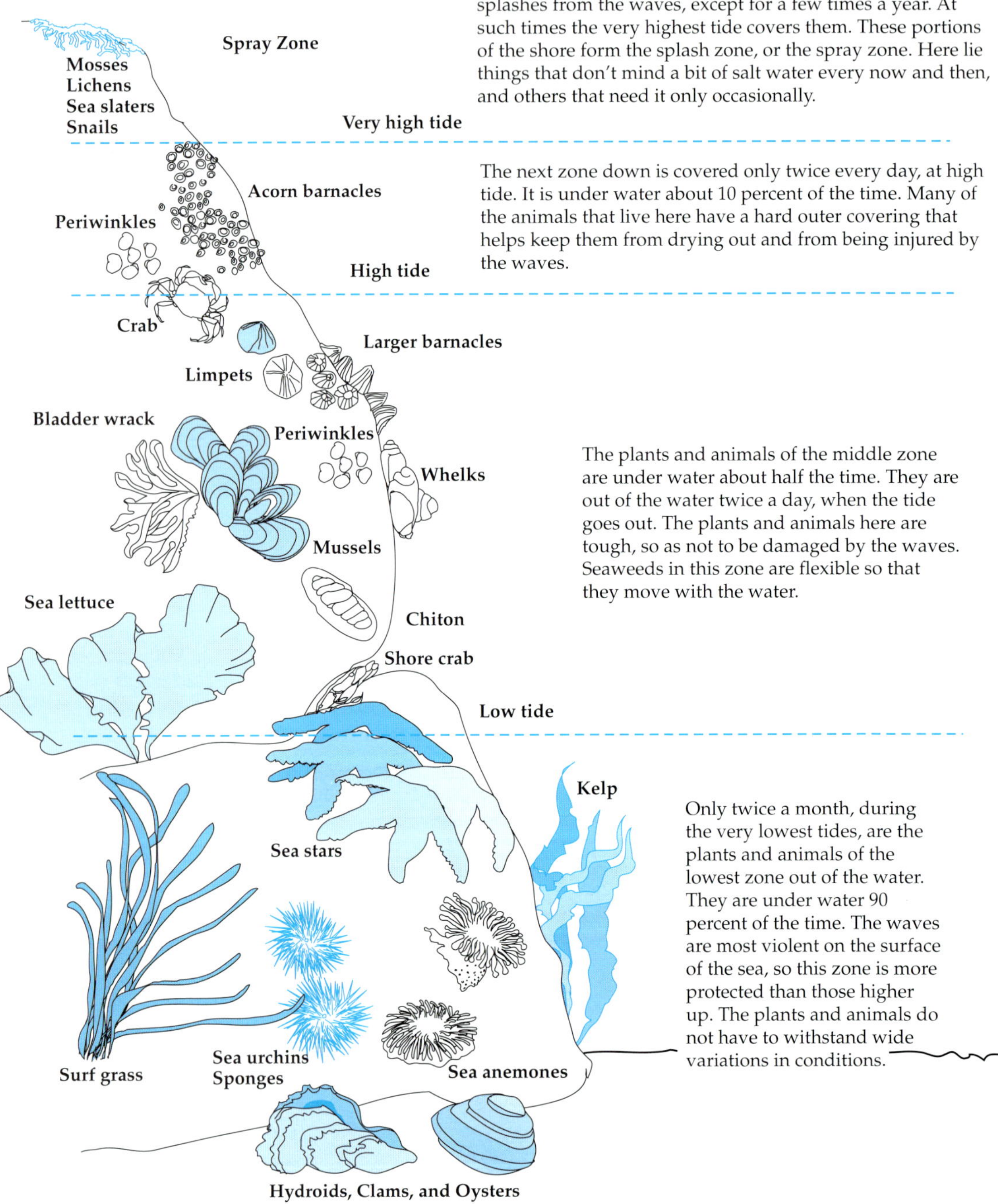

There are some parts of the rocky shore reached only by splashes from the waves, except for a few times a year. At such times the very highest tide covers them. These portions of the shore form the splash zone, or the spray zone. Here lie things that don't mind a bit of salt water every now and then, and others that need it only occasionally.

The next zone down is covered only twice every day, at high tide. It is under water about 10 percent of the time. Many of the animals that live here have a hard outer covering that helps keep them from drying out and from being injured by the waves.

The plants and animals of the middle zone are under water about half the time. They are out of the water twice a day, when the tide goes out. The plants and animals here are tough, so as not to be damaged by the waves. Seaweeds in this zone are flexible so that they move with the water.

Only twice a month, during the very lowest tides, are the plants and animals of the lowest zone out of the water. They are under water 90 percent of the time. The waves are most violent on the surface of the sea, so this zone is more protected than those higher up. The plants and animals do not have to withstand wide variations in conditions.

Wetlands and Estuaries

Wetlands include swamps, bogs, marshes, coastal lagoons, estuaries, and mangroves. They have many different names and are found on every continent except Antarctica. Coastal wetlands have characteristics of land and ocean ecosystems. Their plants and animals are adapted to wet and salty conditions.

People have tended to see wetlands as dangerous places where you can be swallowed up by mud or crocodiles, or eaten alive by mosquitoes, and where nothing useful will grow. This is far from the truth, but because they have not been valued in their natural state, vast areas of wetlands in the world have been lost: they have been deliberately filled in, cleared, drained, or subjected to flood control. It is thought that in the United States, the total area of wetlands (inland wetlands as well as coastal ones) is half what it was 200 years ago.

Wetlands have gently moving tides and small, if any, waves. Snails slowly furrow the surface of the mud. Crabs scuttle for cover at the salt marsh fringe. Birds probe busily along the edge

Fine mud and calm water are typical of an estuarine system. As the tide comes in, it moves up the channels and covers the rich shellfish beds. Most estuaries have narrow entrances that protect them from wave action. Estuary near Nelson, New Zealand.

of the water. This blend of quiet busyness gives wetlands their charm.

Coastal wetlands protect land from the attack of waves, grow food for plants and animals, keep the water clean in harbors and estuaries, and provide a home for many species of plants and animals, including fish that are important to the fishing industry. They are an essential part of Pacific coastal zones, adding to the beauty and variety of the coastline.

Estuaries

An estuary is the place where the freshwater current of a river or stream meets and mixes with the salty tide of the sea. In many cases, it is a big area where a river wanders over a flat coastal plain, dividing into many branches that flood a huge area. Marshes form on the edges of the estuary. Nearly half of the cities in the world are built on or near an estuary.

The salt content of the ocean is about 35 grams to each kilogram of salt water (35 parts per thousand). Freshwater from rivers runs into the ocean and is sometimes carried far out to sea. Freshwater mixes with seawater to form areas of water that are less salty than pure seawater. This is called estuarine water. Any water of less than 33.5 parts per thousand is a mixture of freshwater and seawater. Some plants and animals are able to live only in very salty water, some in freshwater, and some in estuarine water.

Because seawater has salt dissolved in it, there is more matter in a liter of seawater than in a liter of freshwater. We say that the seawater is "denser" than freshwater. When seawater and freshwater come into contact, the denser seawater tends to flow below and the freshwater on top.

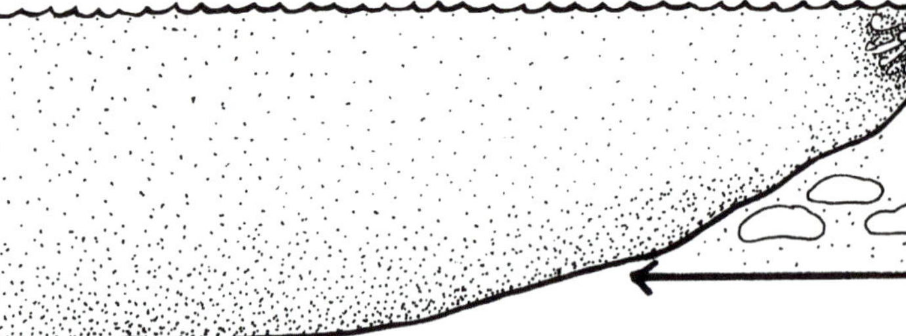

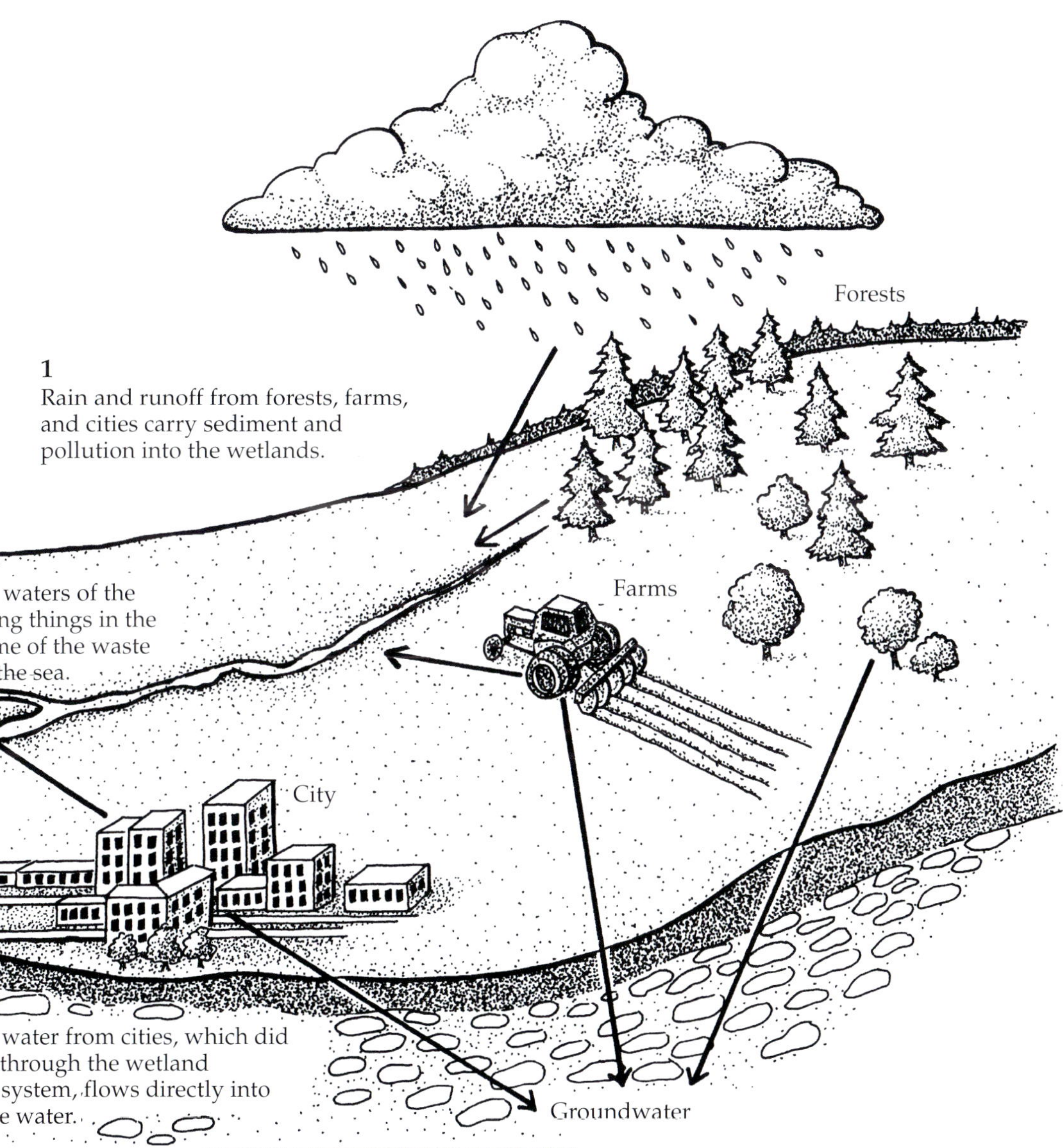

1
Rain and runoff from forests, farms, and cities carry sediment and pollution into the wetlands.

...ie waters of the
...ving things in the
...ome of the waste
...o the sea.

...d water from cities, which did
...s through the wetland
...g system, flows directly into
...ore water.

6
Some water from forests, farms, and cities goes directly into groundwater, carrying pollutants.

Therefore, in most estuaries, the water gets saltier with depth and with distance from the mouth of the river. When the flow of the river is stronger than the push of the tide, the salt water forms a wedge on the bottom. When the tide is stronger, the salt water mixes more evenly with the fresh. There are of course many patterns between the two. Thus, the plants and animals that like different degrees of saltiness can live in a salinity they can toler-

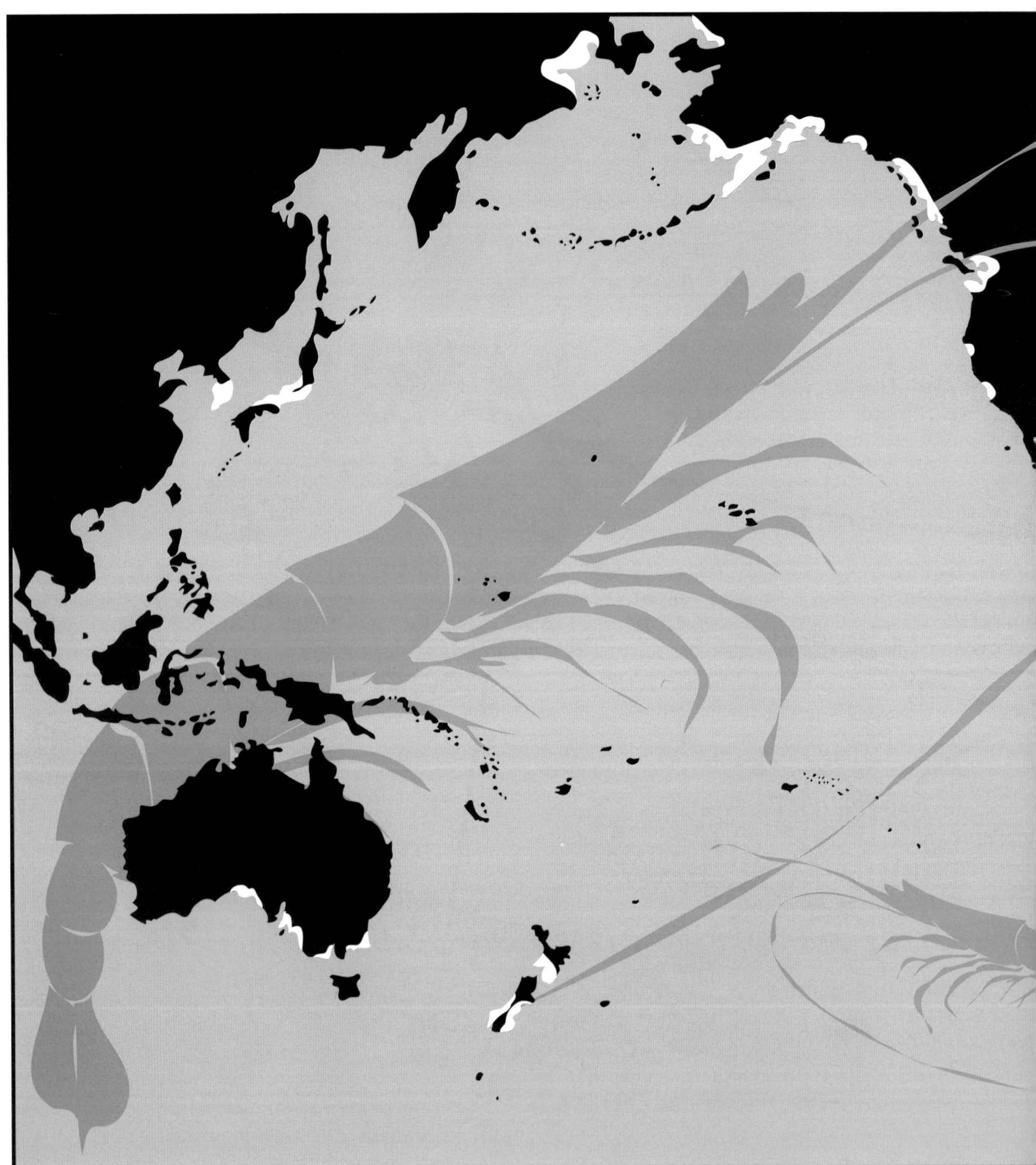

ate and therefore can live in a variety of habitats within the estuary. Not many types of plants and animals can survive in the changing salinity of an estuary, but those that can, grow in profusion because of the nutrients brought down by the river and up by the tide. This is why estuaries are so rich in life.

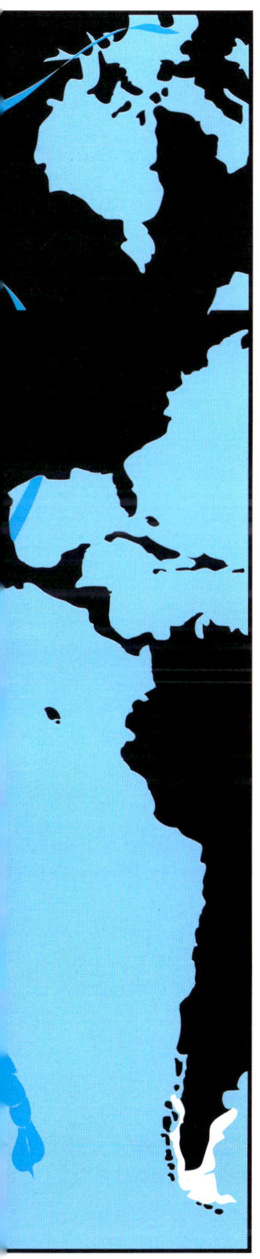

Salt marshes of the Pacific. The white areas show the location of salt marshes.

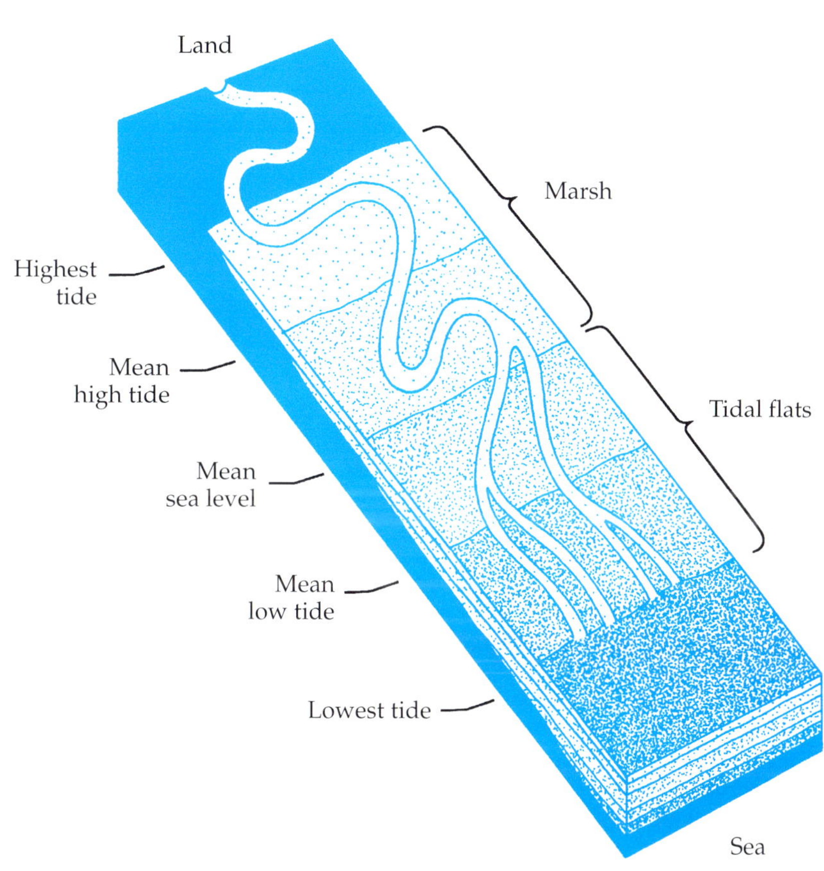

In an estuary, the salt water of the tide meets the freshwater of a river.

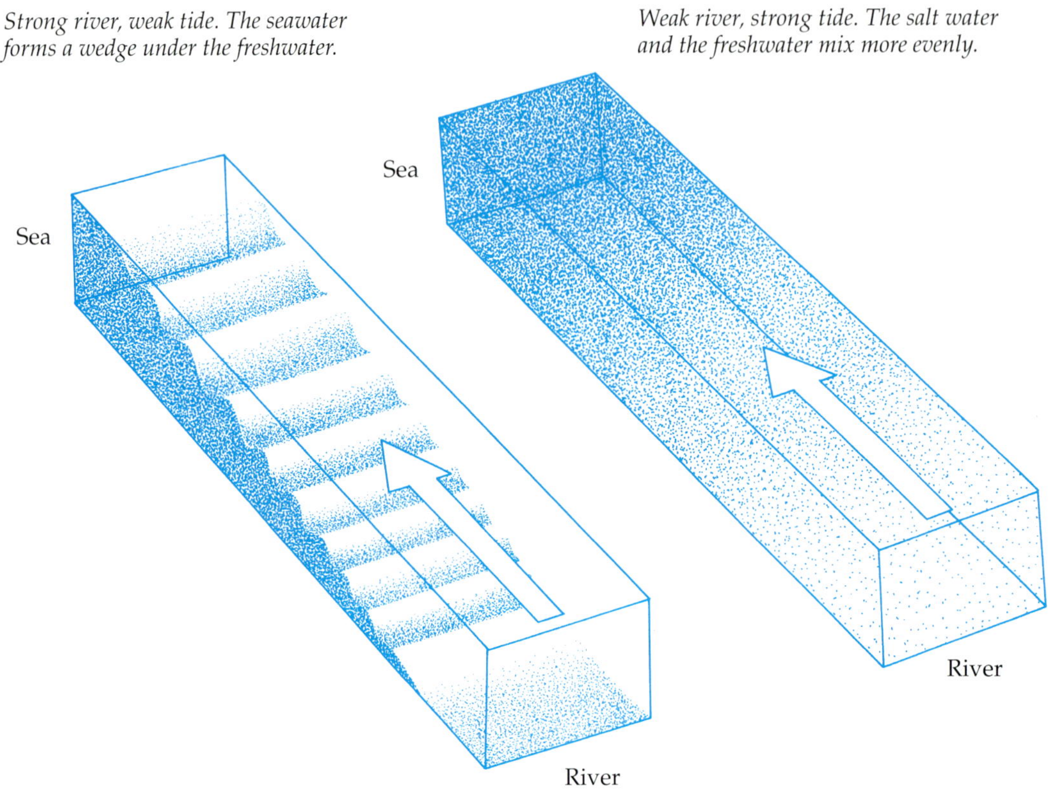

Who Lives Where?

The water of coastal wetlands is never "clean." It is a rich environment for plants to grow in because of the minerals and sediment brought down by rivers and streams and up by the tide, and because shallow water is warm during the day. Where there are lots of plants, animals come to feed. In the wetland, animals find four types of plants providing food for them all the year round: grasses, seaweeds, algae in the mud, and plant plankton. Because there is so much food, wetlands are good nurseries for sea creatures: oysters, crabs, shrimp, and many types of fish. Many of them are important to human beings.

Estuaries, marshes, lagoons and other wetlands swarm with life: plankton, algae, crustaceans, fish, shellfish, stingrays, octopuses, sponges, oysters, grasses, seaweeds, wading birds, crocodiles, waterfowl, rats, cats, and insects. Wetlands are the most productive part of the coastal zone, after mangroves and coral reefs. For this reason wetlands, swamps, marshes, estuaries, and coastal lagoons need to be preserved and protected.

Where Life Is Hard

Although plants and animals thrive in coastal wetlands, their life there is not easy. They face problems that plants and animals living in freshwater, in the ocean, or on land do not have.

- *Not enough air.* Animals and plants living in the mud may have difficulty getting oxygen. In warm water, the oxygen dissolved in the water will escape; therefore, there may be less oxygen in a wetland than there is in the sea. Also, the waves of the sea trap oxygen. In wetlands, however, there is less wave action than in the sea, and so there is also less oxygen in the water.

- *Too much or too little salt.* The amount of salt in the water changes when the tide comes in and goes out and when streams flood. In summer, as water evaporates in the heat of the sun, the estuarine water becomes salty. Sometimes the wetland dries out completely and living things are left in a dry bed of salt. Plants and animals of coastal wetlands have to be able to survive in salt water, in freshwater, and with no water at all.

- *Variations in light and heat.* Where the water is shallow and clear, light can penetrate deeply and stimulate plant growth. On the other hand, in an estuary where rivers carry large amounts of silt, the cloudy water blocks light and plants find it hard to grow. Because the water is shallow, it warms up faster and it cools down faster than do deeper bodies of water. Thus, plants and animals have to be able to cope with a greater range of temperatures.

- *Predators.* Because wetlands are so full of life, they are also full of animals that hunt and eat other animals. Life is therefore more dangerous. Crocodiles and alligators, for instance, live in some tropical and subtropical wetlands. Many birds feed on shellfish and worms.

- *Human beings.* Humans are much more dangerous than crocodiles. They often dump sewage and waste water, poisons and oil into wetlands, killing the plants and animals that live or breed there. Someone who owns a swamp would probably rather own a solid piece of land where a house can be built. People therefore "reclaim" swampland by filling it in and turning it into dry land.

People turn their animals loose to graze in wetlands, and the animals trample through the water and stir up the mud so that the original plants and animals cannot live in the water. The livestock eat the plants and destroy the original balance of the wetland. After a while, different plants start to live there and different animals come to feed on the plants. Water buffalo from Indonesia have had this effect in northern Australia.

Some people think that wetlands are useless land so they use them as rubbish dumps, which destroys them forever. Others use them for speedboat racing, which churns up the water and minces up the plants and animals.

Who eats what in a wetland?

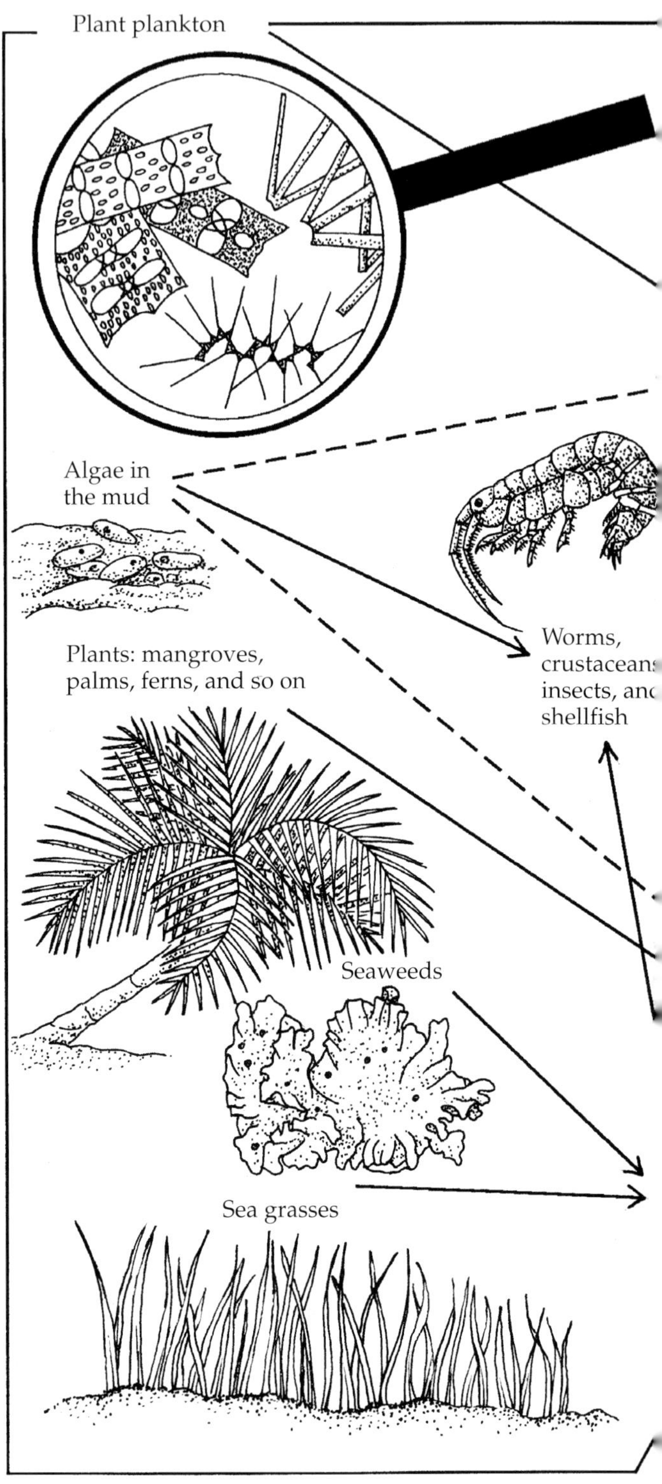

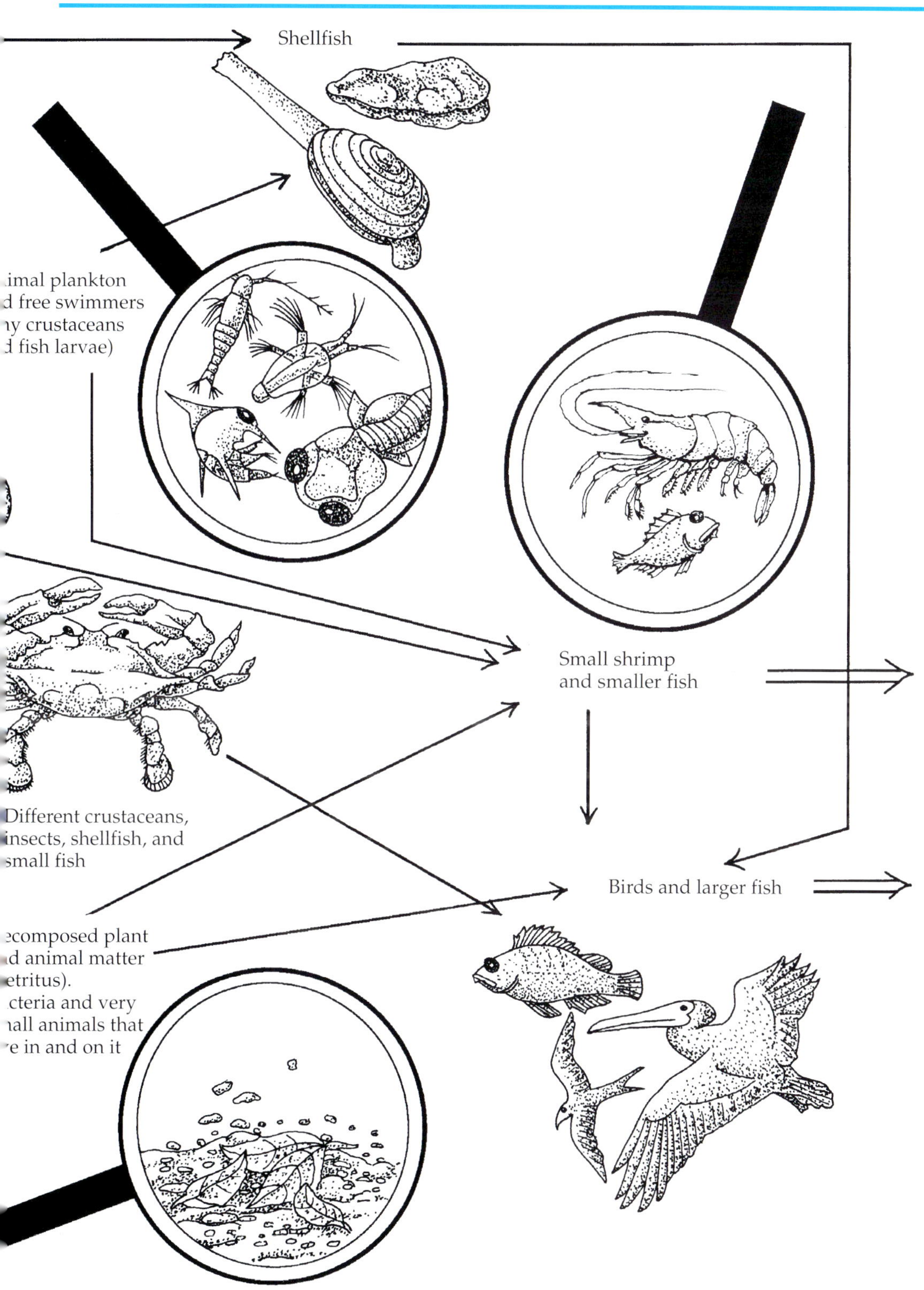

Shellfish
imal plankton
d free swimmers
ny crustaceans
d fish larvae)
Small shrimp
and smaller fish
Different crustaceans,
insects, shellfish, and
small fish
Birds and larger fish
ecomposed plant
d animal matter
etritus).
cteria and very
all animals that
e in and on it

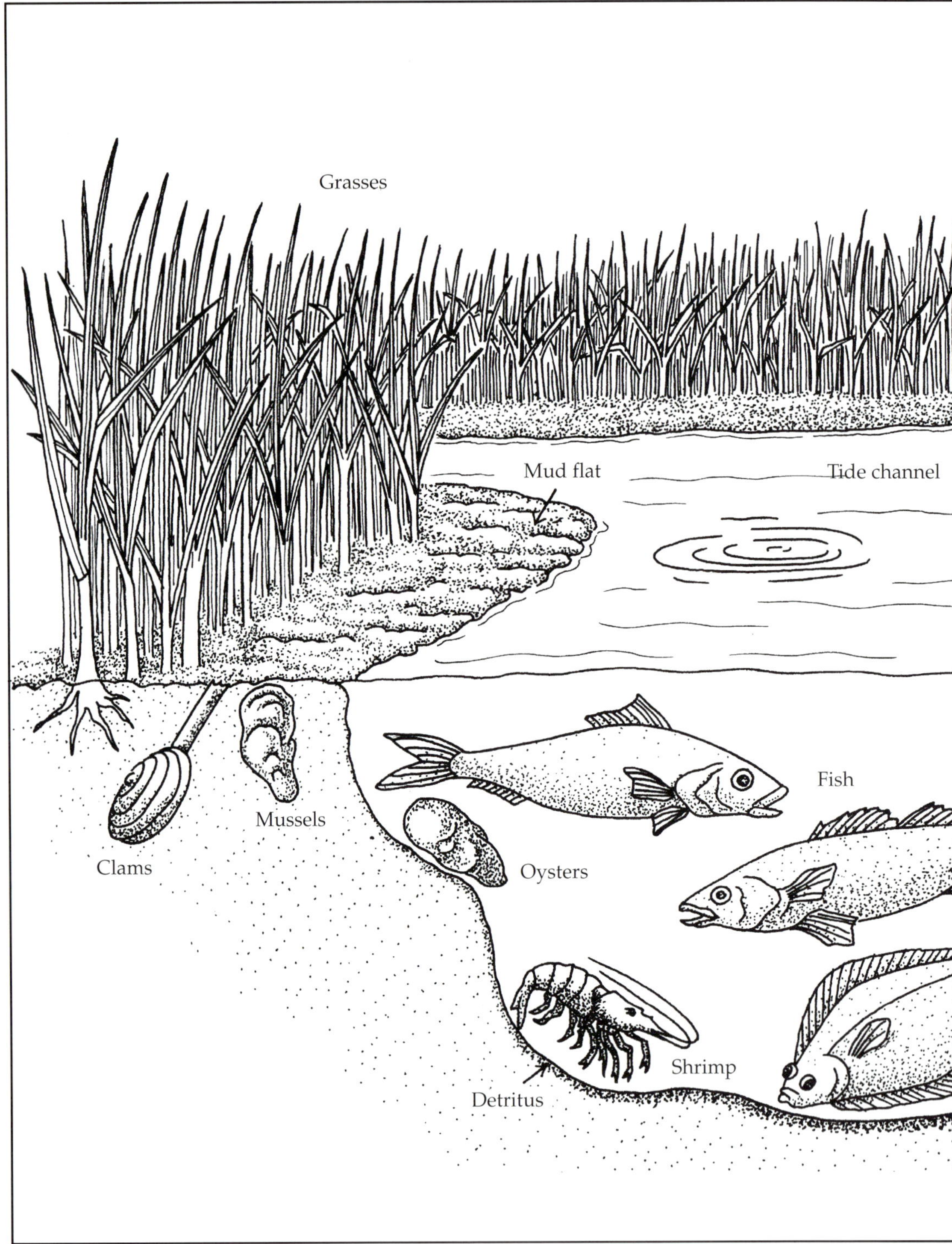

Grasses
Mud flat
Tide channel
Mussels
Clams
Oysters
Fish
Shrimp
Detritus

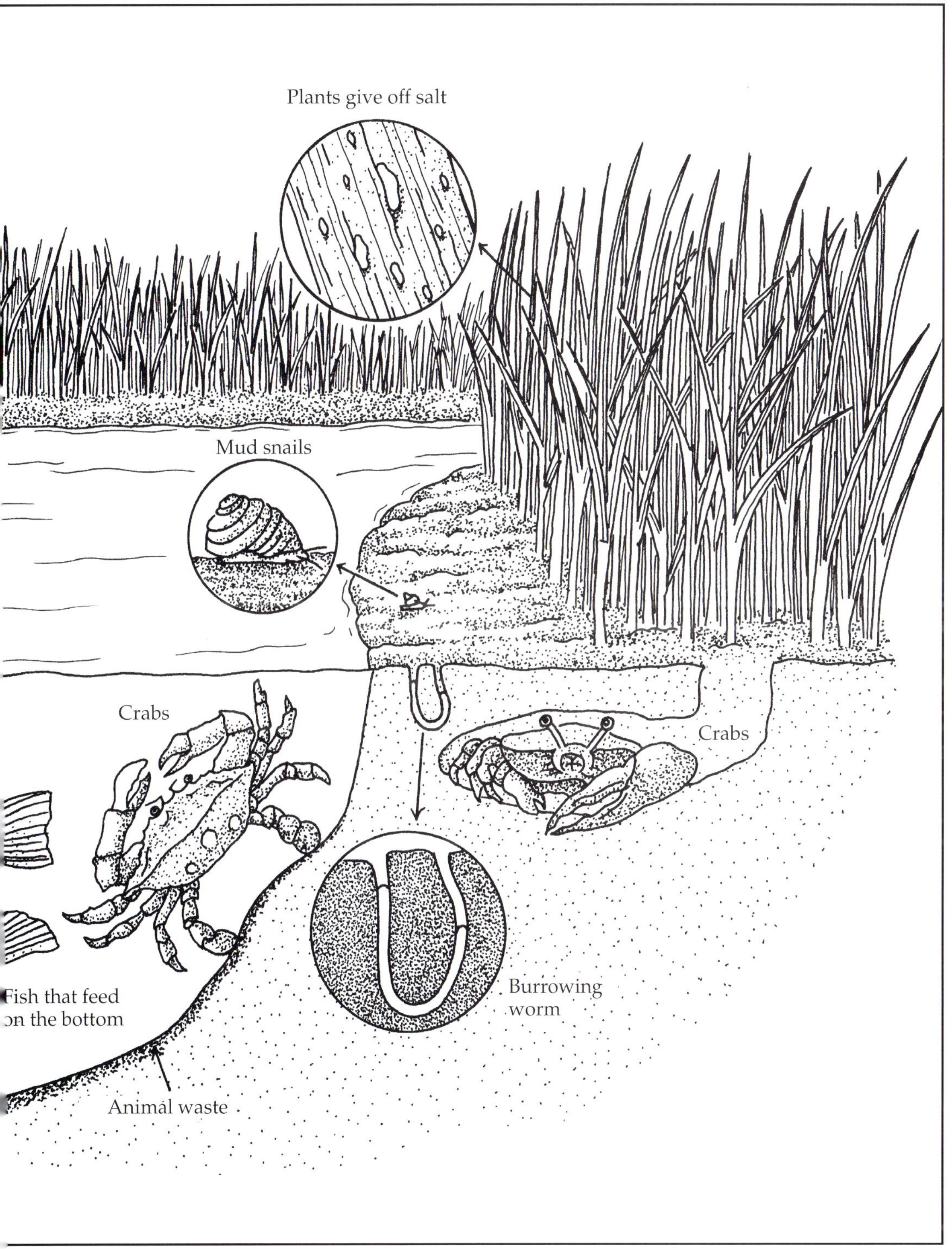

Plants give off salt
Mud snails
Crabs
Crabs
Fish that feed
on the bottom
Animal waste
Burrowing
worm

Lagoons

In the Pacific we tend to think of a lagoon as belonging on a coral island, but there are two types of lagoons. A *coastal lagoon* is an area of salty or brackish water separated from the sea, usually by a sand or gravel barrier. This type of lagoon is found all over the world, from the tropics to the polar regions.

A *coral lagoon* is a lake-like stretch of water enclosed in a coral atoll. These lagoons, of course, occur only in limited areas of the world. Why?

When waves enter shallow water they begin to break. If they break before they reach the shore, they may leave sand and other sediment in a bar offshore. This bar eventually grows into a barrier that may trap water and cause a lagoon to form.

Lagoons are found along coastal plains that slope gently towards the sea. Nearby there is usually a river that carries sediment down to the sea. The sediment is then picked up by waves with help from currents, and deposited to form a barrier.

If we compare the map of coastal lagoons with that of coral reefs we see that for the most part they are found in different areas. There are very few parts of the world where they occur together. This is because coastal lagoons cannot form where there is no moving sand, and moving sand prevents coral from growing.

A coastal lagoon is an area of salt or brackish water separated from the sea, usually by a sand or gravel barrier. This lagoon is sometimes salt and sometimes fresh, depending on the height of the tide and the amount of rain. Trees grow on the barrier, and beyond, you can see the sea. This is a closed lagoon. It was swollen by very heavy rains, but you can see patches of mud where the water is drying up. Kinka Lagoon, Central Queensland.

Most coastal lagoons last less than a thousand years because they are formed by moving sand and sediment. The sediment builds up so much that the lagoon becomes land, or else the sea breaks through and it becomes sea again.

Lagoons are rich in nutrients from the soils washed down by the rivers, from minerals in the seawater, and from plants and algae that grow in the water. Coastal lagoons are therefore among the most organically productive parts of the continental shelf. They are nurseries for young fish, shrimp, and oysters.

In Hawaii and throughout Polynesia, coastal lagoons formed by barriers of coral debris and sand are used as fish ponds for fish farming.

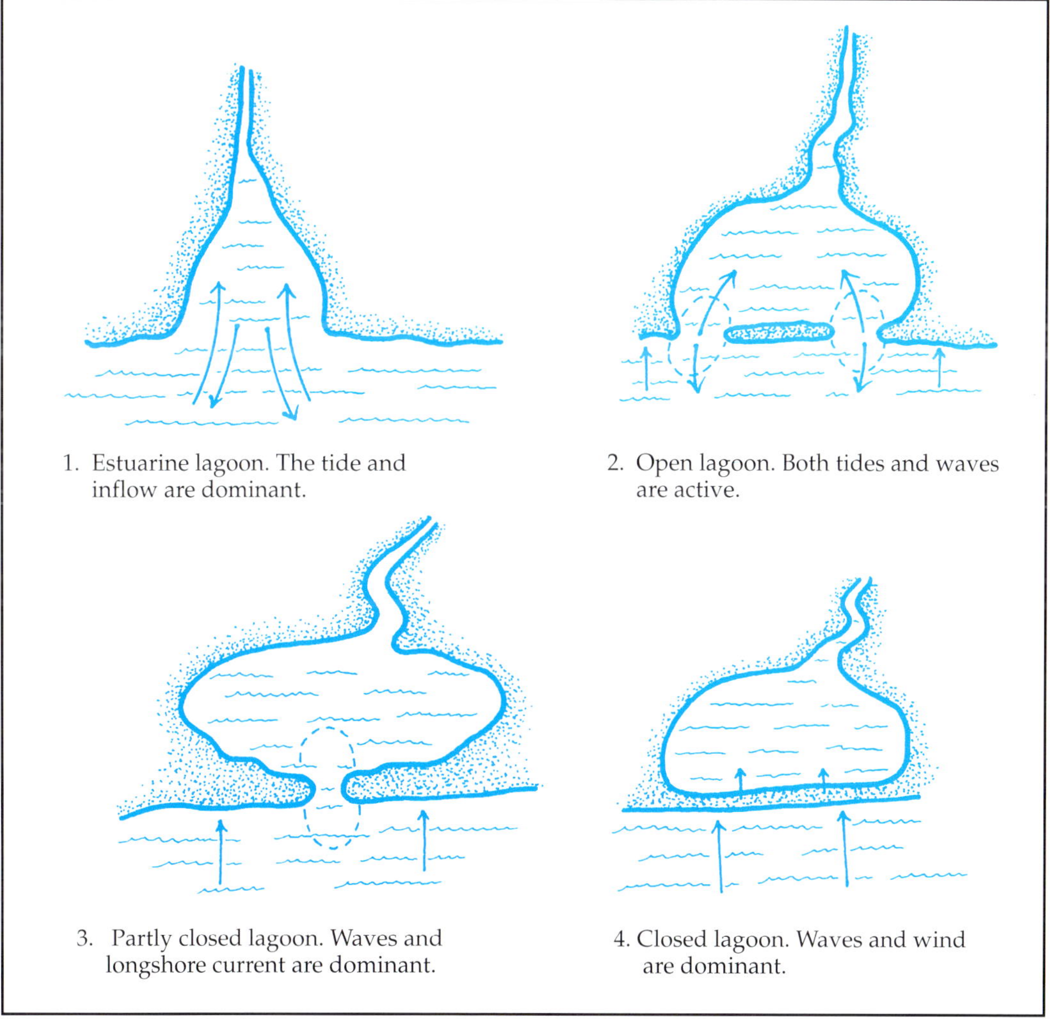

Different ways in which sand or rock—moved by waves, wind, or tide—can trap a mixture of salt water and freshwater.

Marsh grasses grow at the edge of this coastal lagoon in Hawaii.

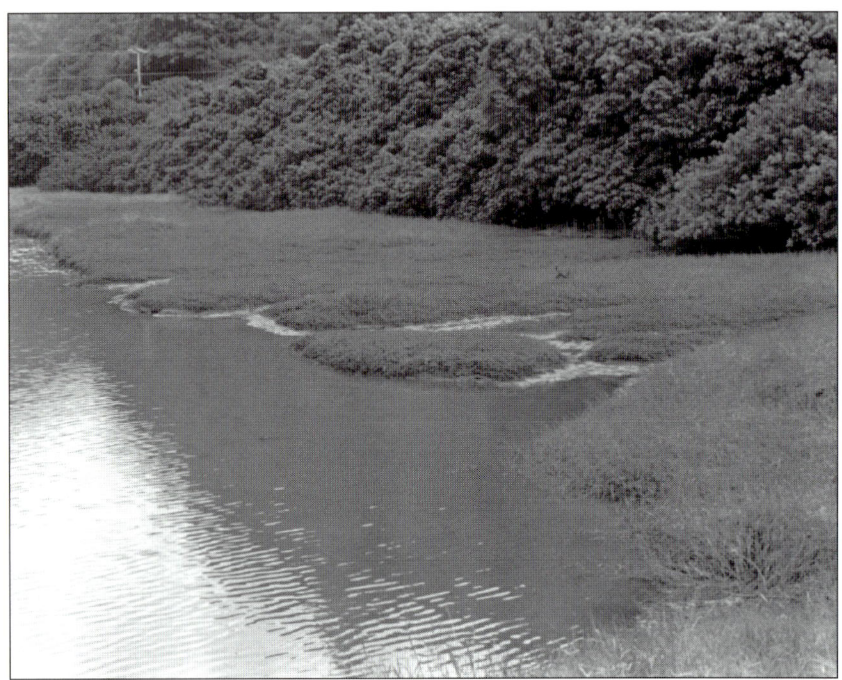

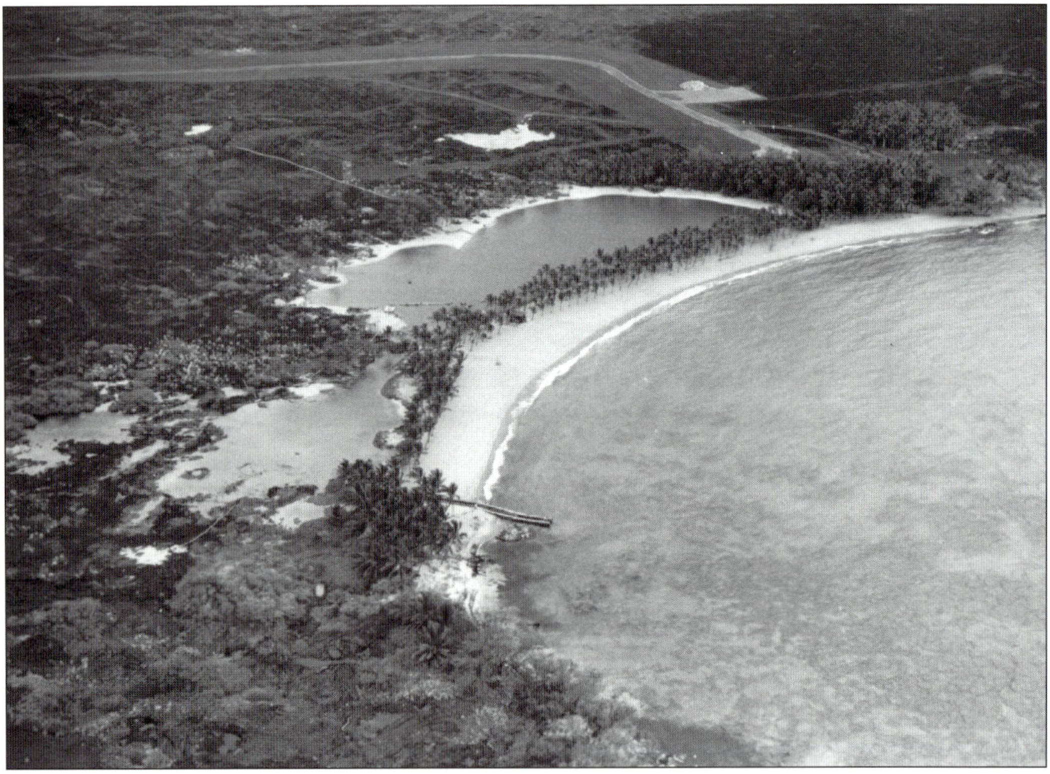

Ancient fish pond in Hawaii. An isolated shore fish pond was usually formed when barrier beaches developed, building a single, elongated sand ridge that paralleled the coast.

Mangroves

The word *mangrove* means above all a type of tree that grows in the tropics. Many mangroves have roots that grow out of the trunk above the ground and prop up the tree. The roots make the tree look like an um brella buried in the mud. The Pacific area has more than 50 types of mangrove trees.

Mangrove trees grow in swamps on the edge of the sea, with their roots in a mixture of salt water and freshwater. Along with the mangrove trees grow many other types of plants, forming a forest or jungle called a *mangrove swamp*. In the Pacific at least 75 types of palms, ferns, and shrubs grow in mangrove areas. Mangrove swamps, sometimes referred to just as

Some mangroves have prop roots. Red mangroves, Rhizophora stylosa.

Some have peg roots, which shoot up like snorkels through the mud. The peg roots help to anchor the plant, and they take in oxygen. Shown here are white mangroves, Avicennia marina. *Mangrove swamps are not very beautiful.*

mangroves, are a type of coastal wetland. They are by far the most productive ocean environment.

Some types of mangroves live in the tropics, but they are also found in the North Island of New Zealand and on the coasts of Victoria in southern Australia. Because of the cool climates, they do not grow very large and are called stunted mangroves. Nearly one-fourth of the Australian coastline is mangrove. In southern China, a project began in the 1960s to save eroded coastal areas by planting mangroves.

Mangrove trees grow where most other plants cannot, in salt swamps. There are several reasons for this.

- They have leaves that are specially adapted to help balance the plant's water and salt.

- They have a network of roots that stop the plant from falling over in the soft, wet mud. Some types of mangroves have roots that push up through the mud like snorkels to take in oxygen.

- They have no seeds. Instead the young plant is protected inside a paperlike case. The case splits open and the baby plant drops, unfolds, and produces roots to anchor itself in the mud. The paper case stops it from getting too much salt.

Mangroves help to purify pollution from urban runoff, so when mangroves near a growing city are cleared away, pollution problems will probably increase.

Mangroves perform special services in the coastal zone.

- They are among the few trees that can grow in areas regularly covered by seawater.

- Their roots catch sediments that flow down from the land and up with the tide. Other plants grow in this sediment, protected by the mangroves, and so a forest or jungle grows up among the mangrove trees.

In this tide channel, the mud is riddled with pellets formed by the sand bubbler crab, which breaks down the mangrove detritus. The detritus, in turn, is food for the other mangrove animals. Statue Beach, Australia.

- In areas where the tide is very strong, or where the waves might wash the soil away, mangrove roots hold the soil together, protecting the coast from erosion.

- They provide shade, a home, and food for a vast number of living things that feed on the mangrove fruit and leaves that have fallen into the water and decayed.

- They are a valuable economic resource for coastal people.

Mangroves in the Pacific

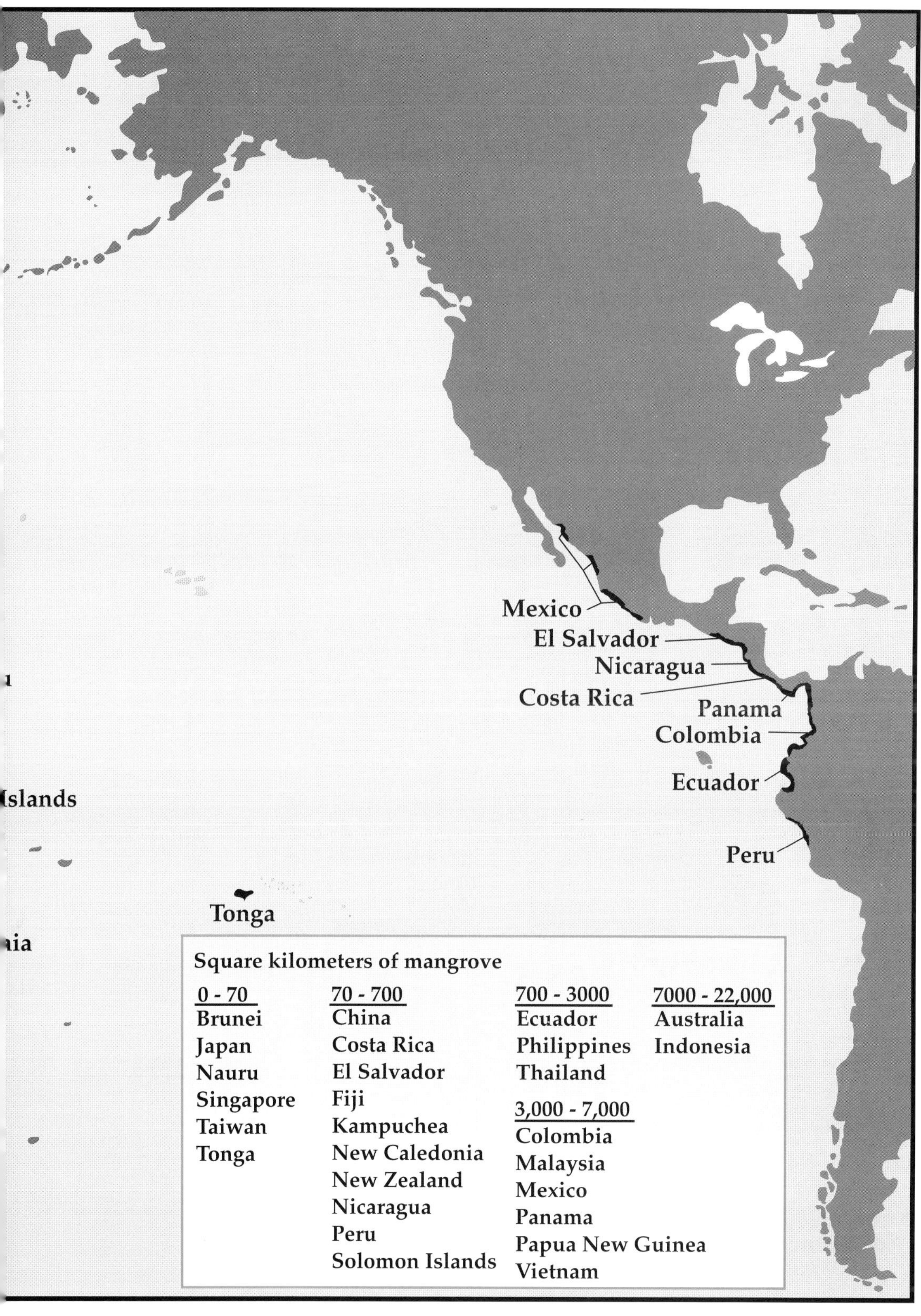

Mexico
El Salvador
Nicaragua
Costa Rica
Panama
Colombia
Ecuador
Peru
Tonga
Islands
1
Square kilometers of mangrove
0 - 70
Brunei
Japan
Nauru
Singapore
Taiwan
Tonga
70 - 700
China
Costa Rica
El Salvador
Fiji
Kampuchea
New Caledonia
New Zealand
Nicaragua
Peru
Solomon Islands
700 - 3000
Ecuador
Philippines
Thailand
3,000 - 7,000
Colombia
Malaysia
Mexico
Panama
Papua New Guinea
Vietnam
7000 - 22,000
Australia
Indonesia

A mangrove seed unfolds.

Who eats what in a mangrove forest?

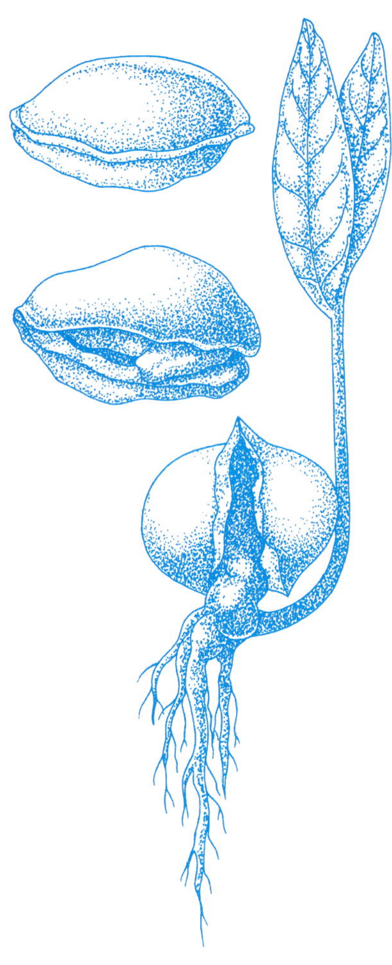

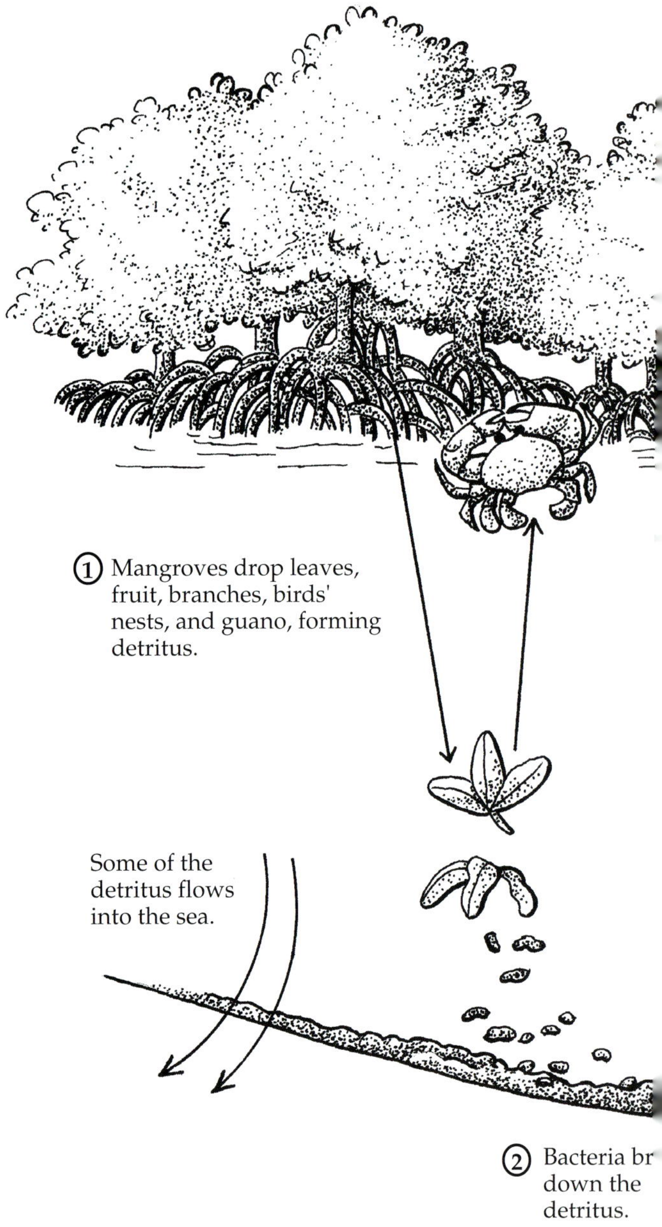

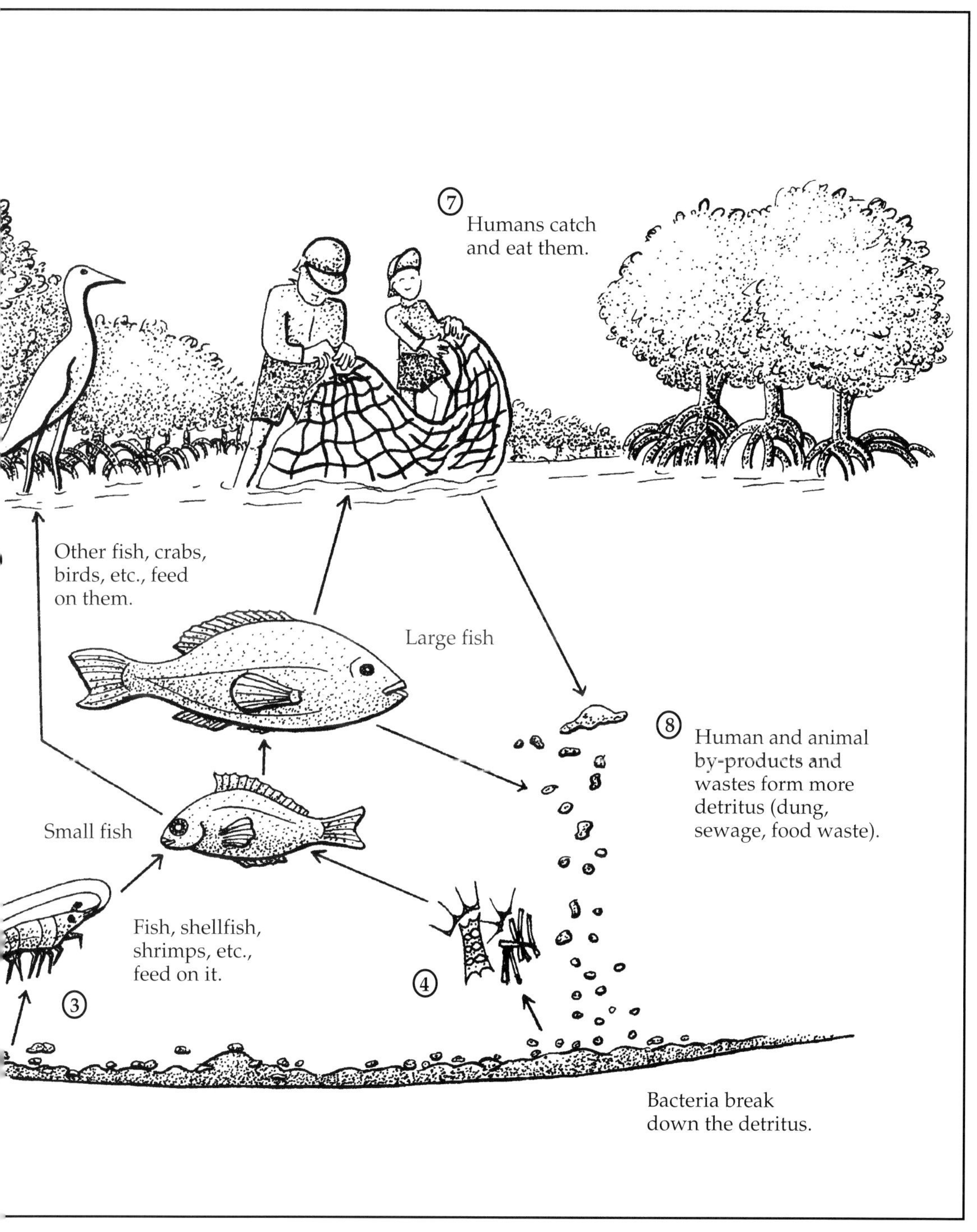

7 Humans catch and eat them.
Other fish, crabs, birds, etc., feed on them.
Large fish
Small fish
Fish, shellfish, shrimps, etc., feed on it.
3
4
8 Human and animal by-products and wastes form more detritus (dung, sewage, food waste).
Bacteria break down the detritus.

Some Products from a Mangrove Forest

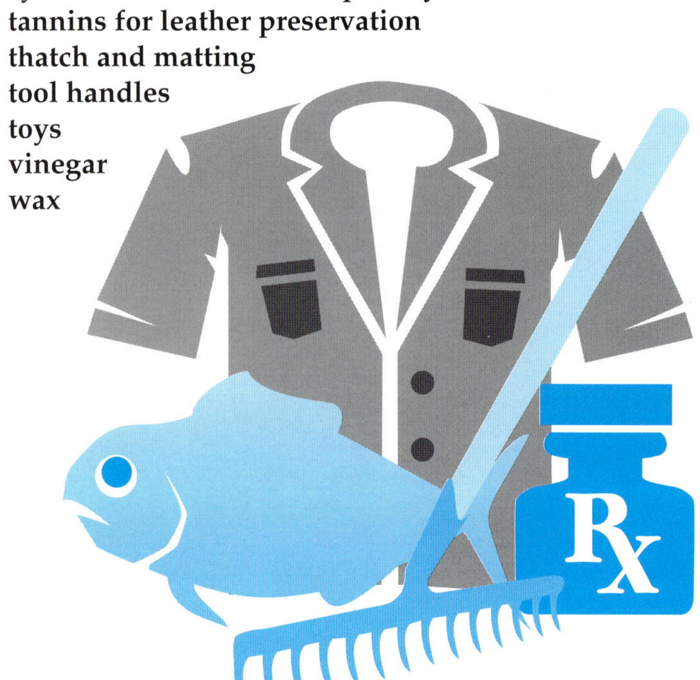

alcohol
condiments from bark
cooking oil
dessert topping
dye
firewood
fish
fish poison
fishing equipment
honey
incense
lumber
matchsticks
medicines
paper
sugar

synthetic fibers (for example, rayon)
tannins for leather preservation
thatch and matting
tool handles
toys
vinegar
wax

Coral Reefs and Atolls

Animal, Vegetable, or Mineral?

Until the year 1723, coral was believed to be a plant. Between 1723 and 1821 there was a great deal of scientific discussion about what coral could be. The idea that it was composed of animals was put forward and quickly rejected. Some rebels thought it was rock. Finally, in 1821, naturalists accepted that coral is a living collection of many generations of animals that form a colony. In fact, it can be argued that a large coral reef is the biggest living thing in the world.

The animal that forms coral is called a polyp. Its structure is rather like that of a jellyfish. The jellyfish swims in the sea, but the coral polyp attaches itself to a hard surface. Most types of coral polyps have a diameter of less than 3 millimeters.

The hard coral polyp produces a cup made of the same material as limestone. This limestone skeleton remains after the animal dies and forms the stonelike coral we often see out of the water. The bodies of the polyps connect with each other, hiding

There are hundreds of different kinds of coral with many different shapes, such as these branching corals.

their white skeletons. Thus, "live" coral under the water is brightly colored by the bodies of the living animals. Different kinds of hard corals build up colonies in different shapes.

There are soft corals too. They do not have a hard, external skeleton, but when they die, their bodies break down and their hard remains pile up to form another sort of limestone. Since hard and soft corals often live together, both contribute to the formation of reefs.

Reef corals feed on the waste dropped by fish and other sea creatures and on very small plants and animals that float in the ocean currents. Once the reef gets these foods, it recycles them quickly and with little waste, over and over again, through a food chain. A lot of food is produced in coral reefs; by comparison the surrounding sea produces little.

Reefs are built by two kinds of organisms: corals, which are tiny animals, and calcareous algae, which are plants containing calcium. They take in seawater containing food and calcium. They attach themselves to shells, to rocks, and to each other, and

Cross section of a coral polyp

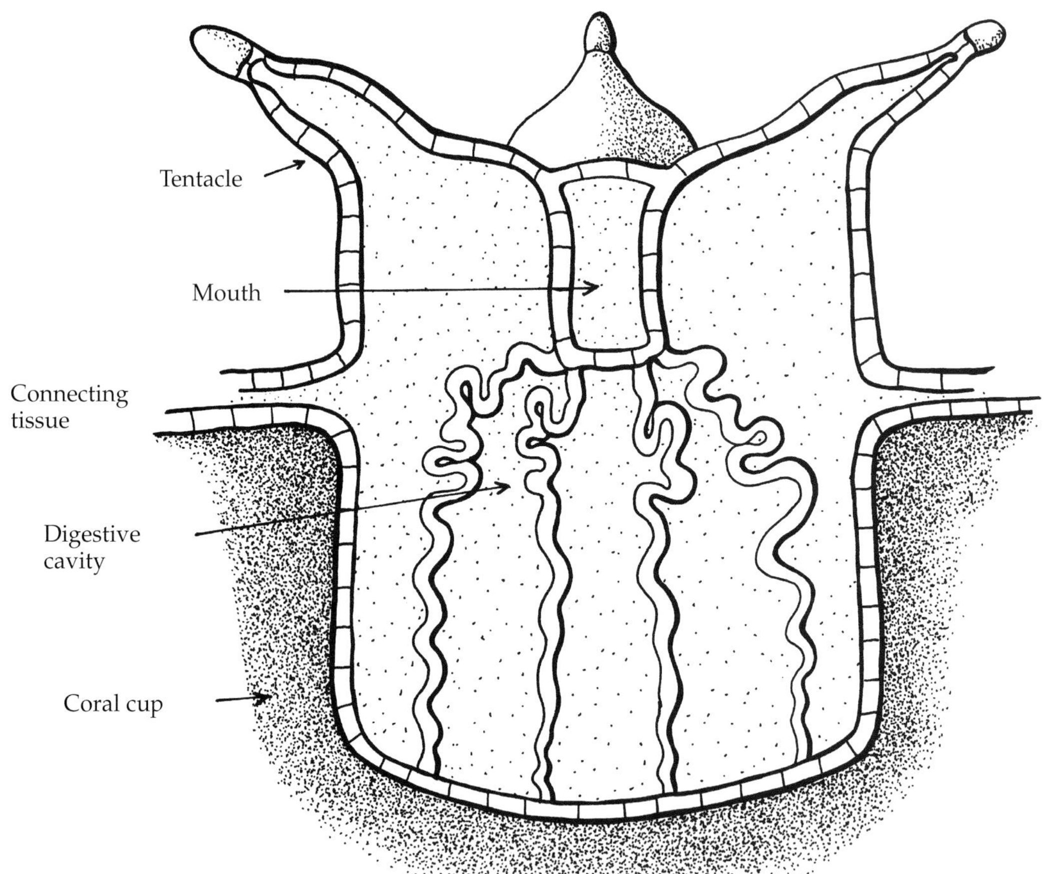

after they die, their calcium remains behind, cementing the whole together into a reef. New reef life settles there when they die. Each new generation lives on the remains of the old reef. So the reef is built up.

Corals have a very complicated relationship with tiny plants that live within them. Each helps the other. The plants provide food for the coral and help the coral polyps produce their skeletons. The coral gives the plants a place to live and makes materials that the plants need for photosynthesis. Animals can live for quite a long time without sunlight, but plants will die very quickly. Although reef-building corals are animals, they need sunlight for the tiny plants that live inside them.

A variety of coral types

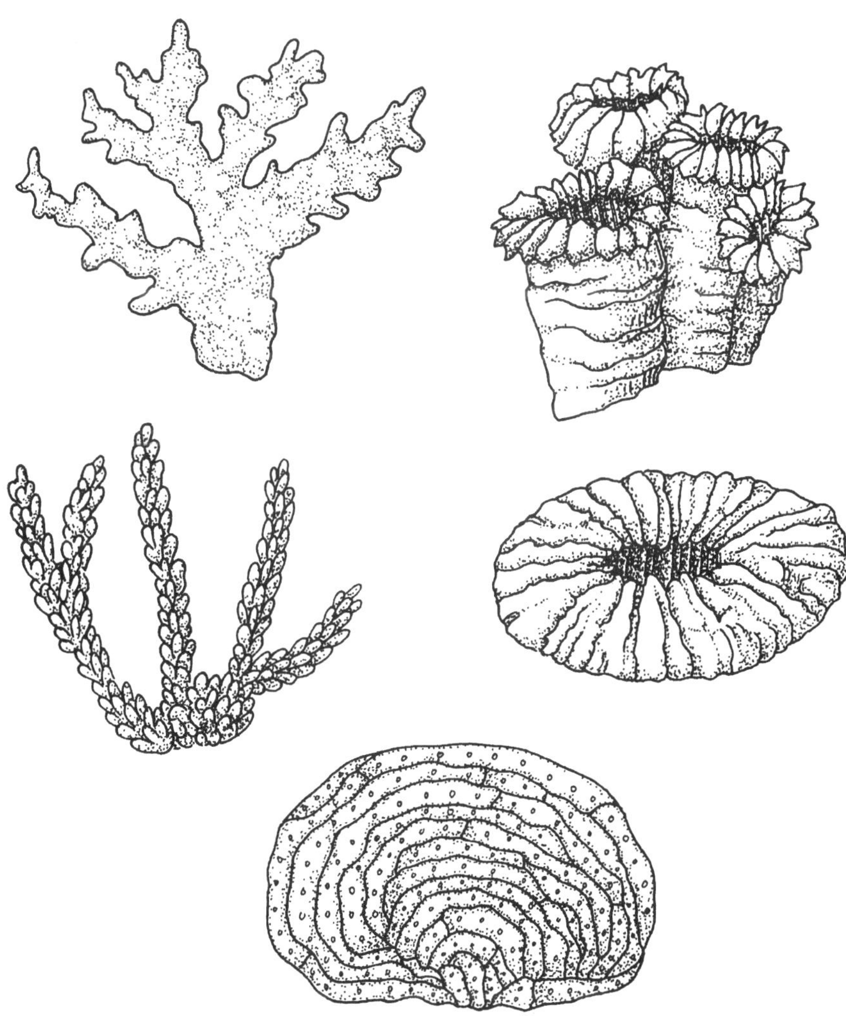

The three basic types of coral reefs

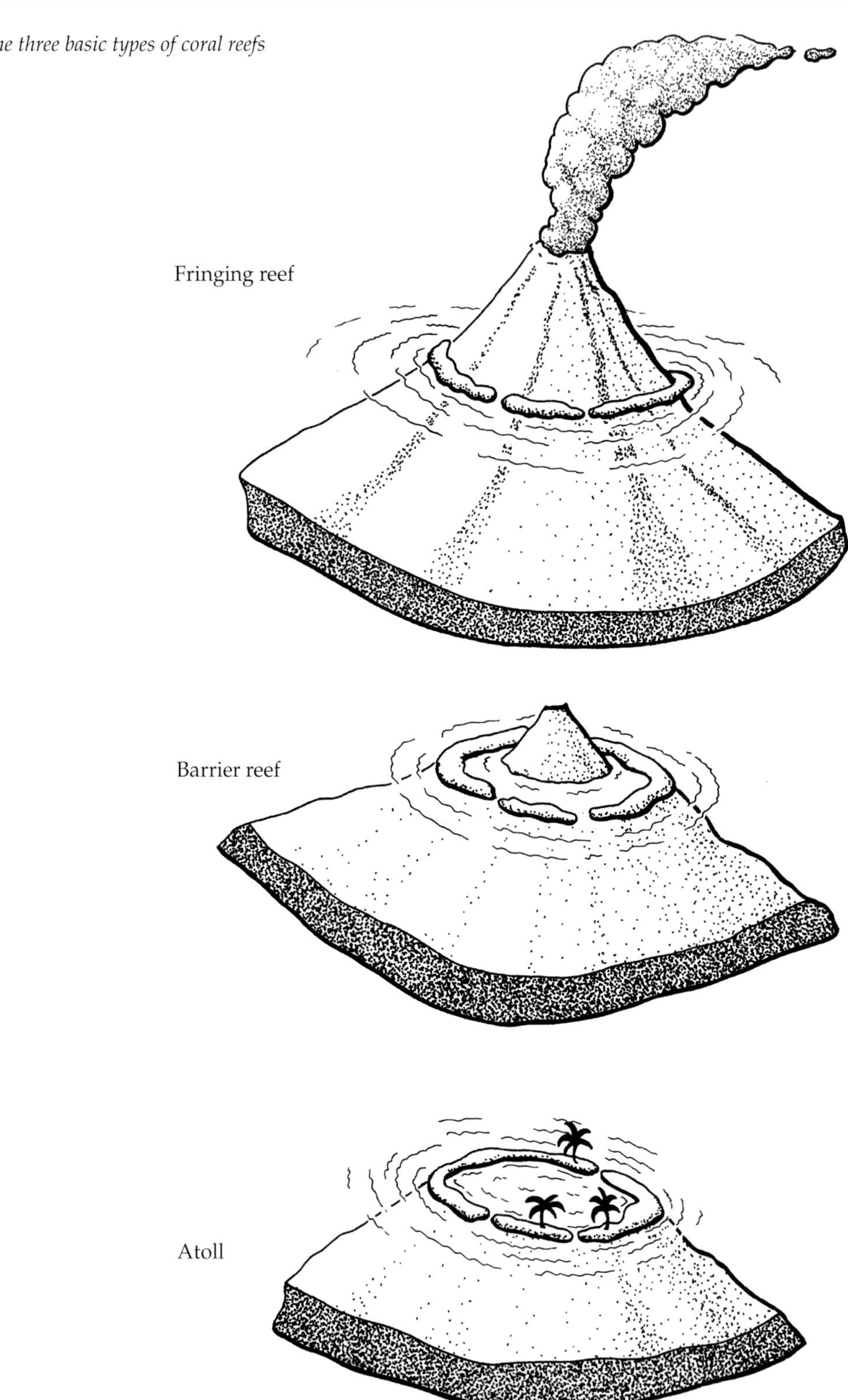
Fringing reef
Barrier reef
Atoll

Charles Darwin's Atolls

About atolls, the naturalist, Charles Darwin, in 1842, wrote

> every one must be struck with astonishment, when he first beholds one of these vast rings of coral-rock, often many leagues in diameter, here and there surmounted by a low verdant island with dazzling white shores, bathed on the outside by the foaming breakers of the ocean, and on the inside surrounding a calm expanse of water, which, from reflection, is generally of a bright but pale green color. The naturalist will feel this astonishment more deeply after having examined the soft and almost gelatinous bodies of these apparently insignificant creatures [coral], and when he knows that the solid reef increases only on the outer edge, which day and night is lashed by the breakers of an ocean never at rest.
>
> —*The Structure and Distribution of Coral Reefs*

Darwin's sketch of Whitsunday Island, a "lagoon-island," or atoll

Coral can grow only in warm water just below the surface of the sea, and yet the coral skeletons of an atoll may go down a thousand meters.

How did an atoll come to be? Originally, a volcano rose out of the sea, a steep island with a fringing reef like a necklace.

Then the mountain eroded or started sinking into the sea. The coral grew toward the surface as the mountain sank, forming a barrier reef with a lagoon inside it.

The mountain sank below the sea or eroded completely, but the coral grew higher and higher, forming an atoll.

Coral sand and organic matter built up on the atoll, plants started to grow, and the low green islands with the dazzling white shores were formed, surrounding the calm green water of the lagoon.

Two views of Bora Bora, Tahiti, as drawn by Darwin

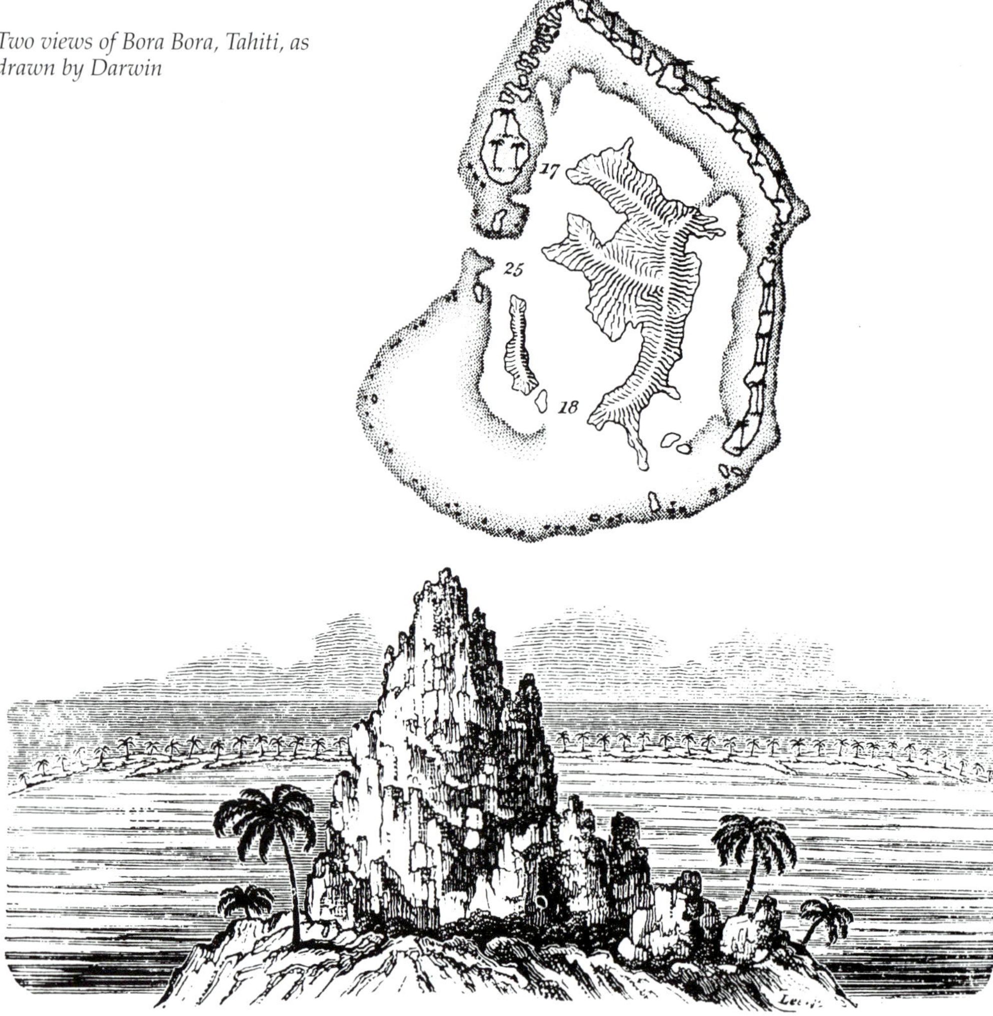

Distribution of Corals

Reef-building corals need sunlight and water at 20 degrees Celsius and above. Thus, they live between 30 degrees north and south of the equator and where the water is clear and shallow, such as on continental shelves, around islands, and on undersea mountains. Most grow no farther than 15 meters below the surface, but some can survive down to 60 meters. Rivers dump sand and soil in the ocean. If this material covers corals, they cannot dig themselves out, and they are smothered. Coral therefore does not develop near the mouths of large rivers. This is why in the Pacific, coral is found mostly around islands, which do not have big rivers, and on the Great Barrier Reef of Australia, which does not have much water.

Some types of corals live in colder waters. They are found, for example, off the North Island of New Zealand and in Sydney Harbour. The southernmost coral in the world is found in the waters near Perth, in Western Australia.

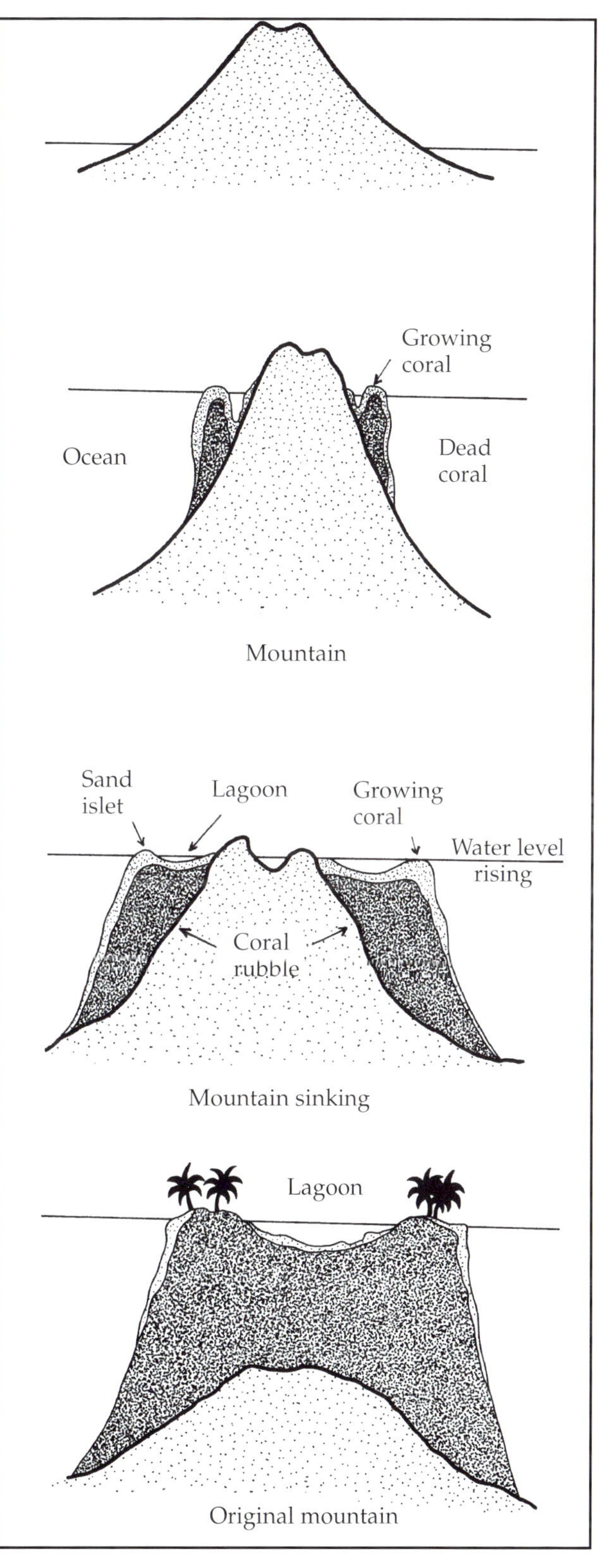

Formation of an atoll

Distribution of coral in the Pacific. The lines are isotherms, which show water temperature in degrees Celcius. The numbers near the place names show the number of different types of coral known to live there.

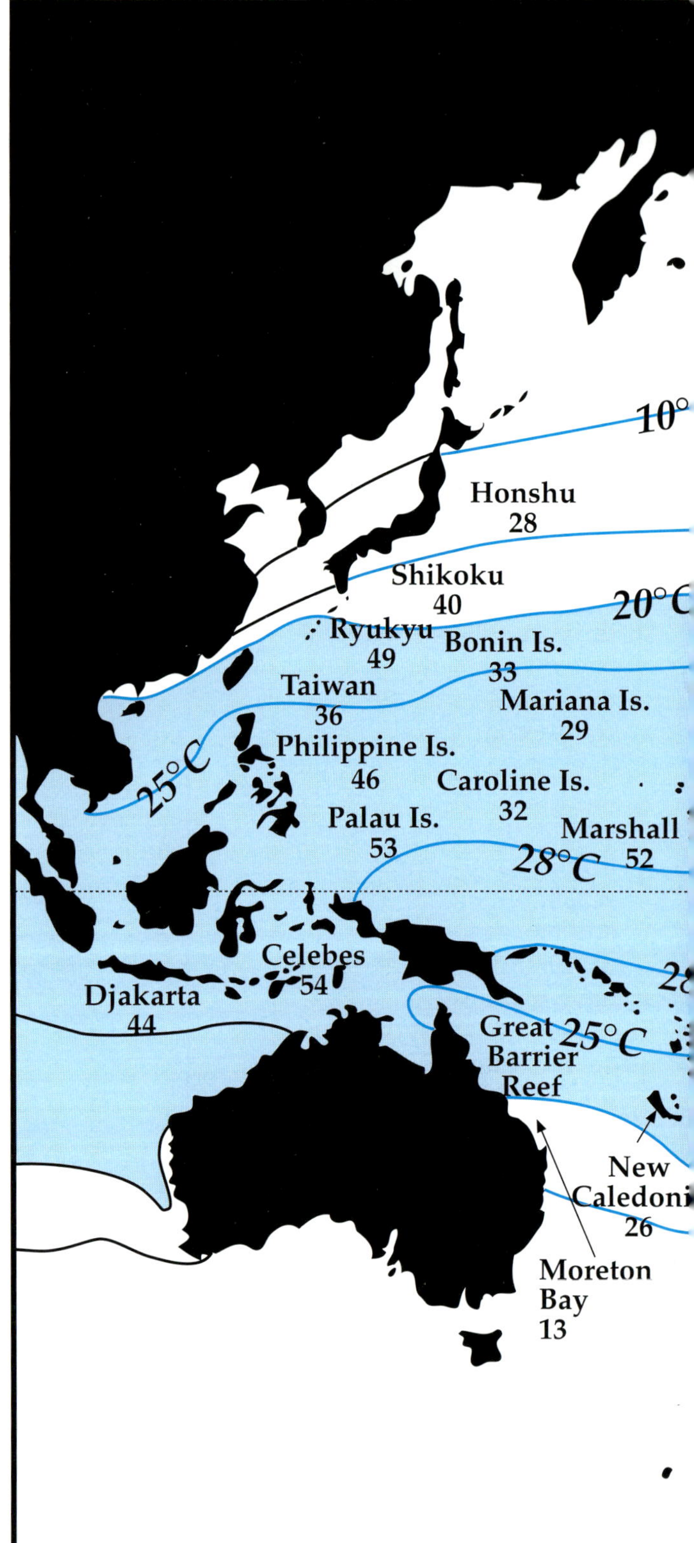

10°
Honshu
28
Shikoku
40
20°C
Ryukyu
49
Bonin Is.
33
Taiwan
36
Mariana Is.
29
Philippine Is.
46
Caroline Is.
32
Palau Is.
53
Marshall
28°C 52
25°C
Celebes
54
Djakarta
44
28
Great 25°C
Barrier
Reef
New
Caledoni
26
Moreton
Bay
13

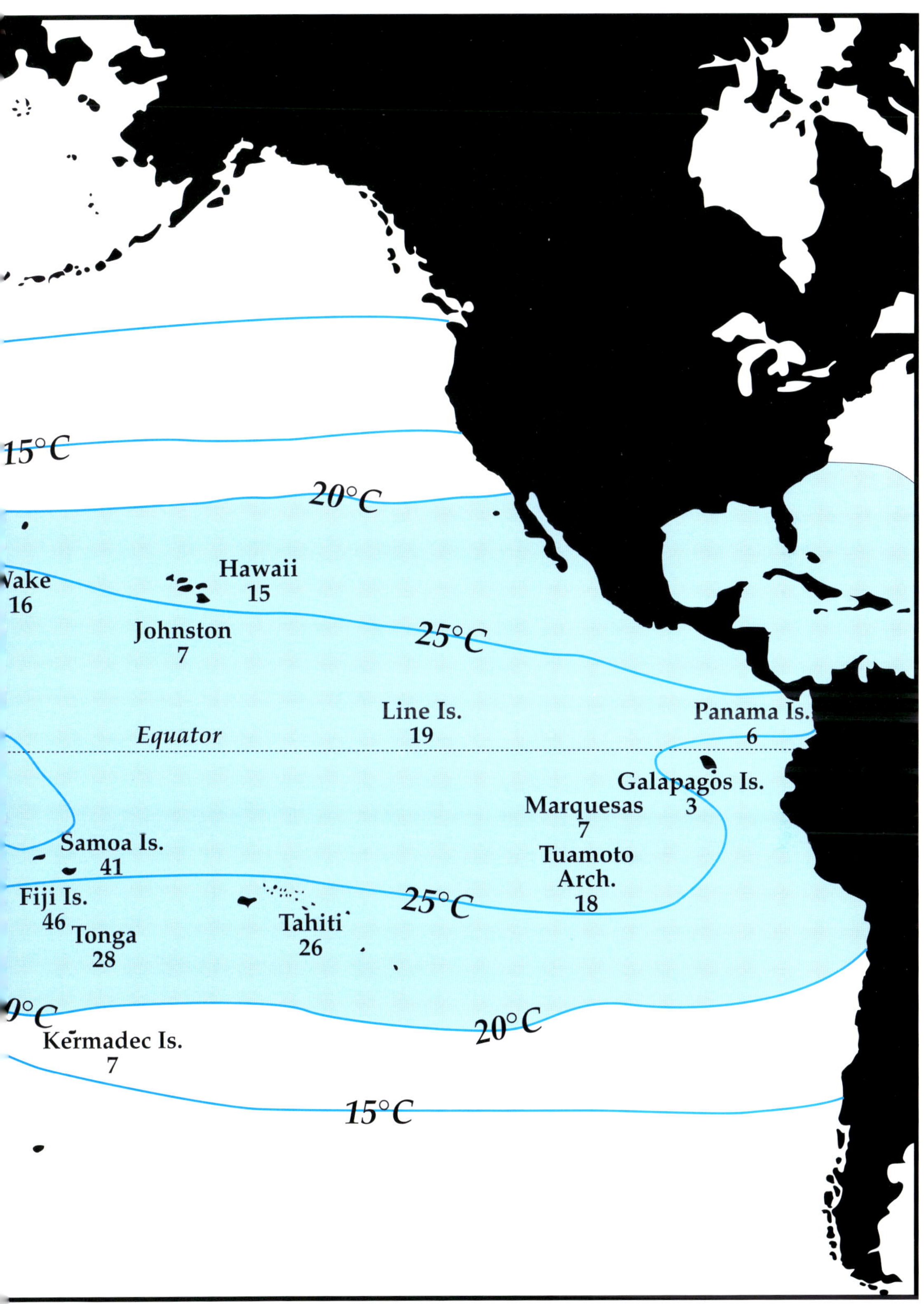

15°C
20°C
25°C
25°C
20°C
15°C
Wake
16
Hawaii
15
Johnston
7
Line Is.
19
Panama Is.
6
Equator
Galapagos Is.
3
Marquesas
7
Samoa Is.
41
Tuamoto
Arch.
18
Fiji Is.
46
Tonga
28
Tahiti
26
Kermadec Is.
7

Harbors and Cities

B oats and ships need deep, sheltered water near shore so that they can anchor without running aground, out of danger from the winds of the open sea. In such places, people build wharves and start trading, and so cities grow up nearby. Protected waters for harbors may be found at the ends of bays or sounds, in lagoons or estuaries, or even in extinct volcanos. Sometimes artificial harbors have been built because, for a variety of reasons, cities have grown up on exposed coasts.

In the twentieth century, cities have grown as they have never grown before. A hundred years ago, cities were full of horses. Now they are designed for cars. Huge ships carry food, oil, coal, and manufactured goods between ports, satisfying the needs of the people. These enormous ports are a new part of the Pacific coastal zone. As their numbers and size increase, we will have to learn how to solve the problems they bring with them.

Pacific Rim cities with a population over 2 million. In most cases, the figures shown are those for the metropolitan areas themselves and do not include the many smaller cities that grow up around major cities. An asterisk (*) beside a population figure means that the smaller cities have been included.

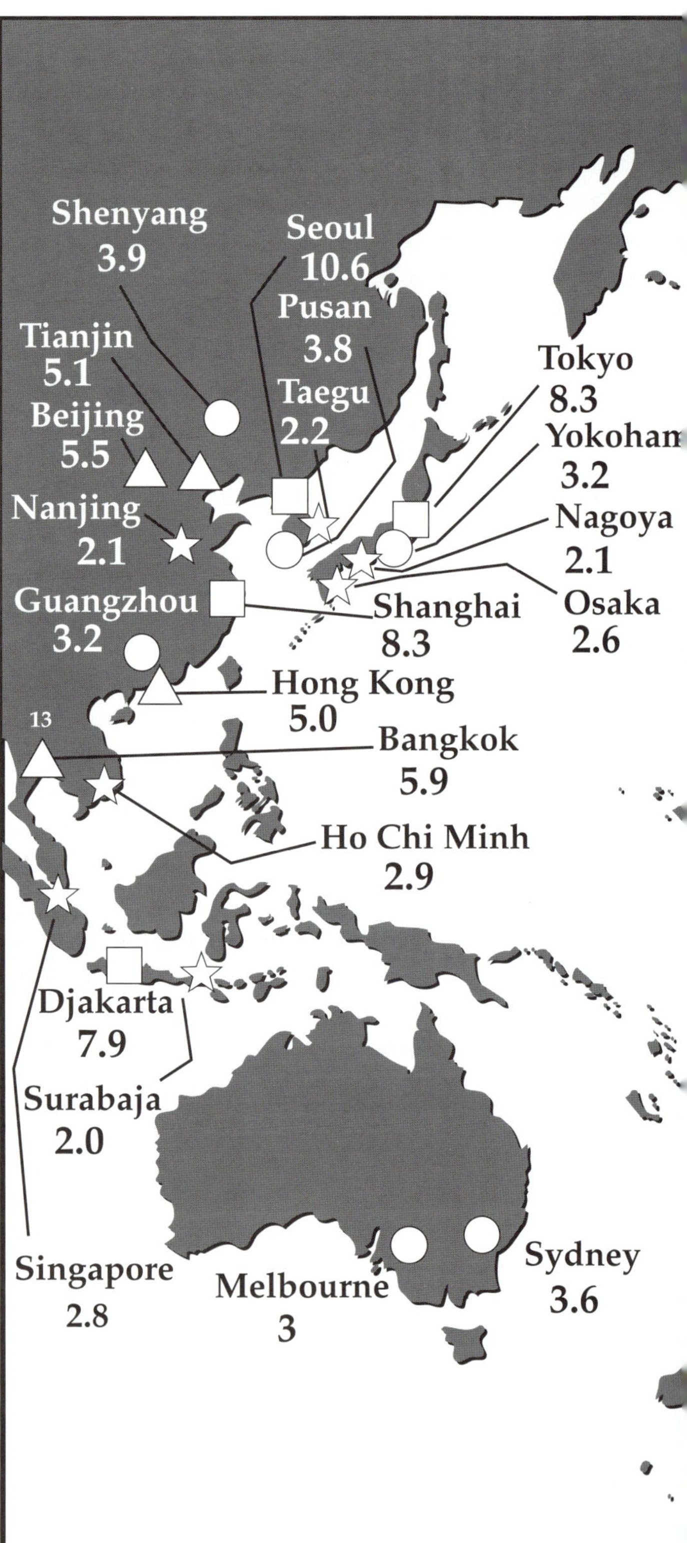

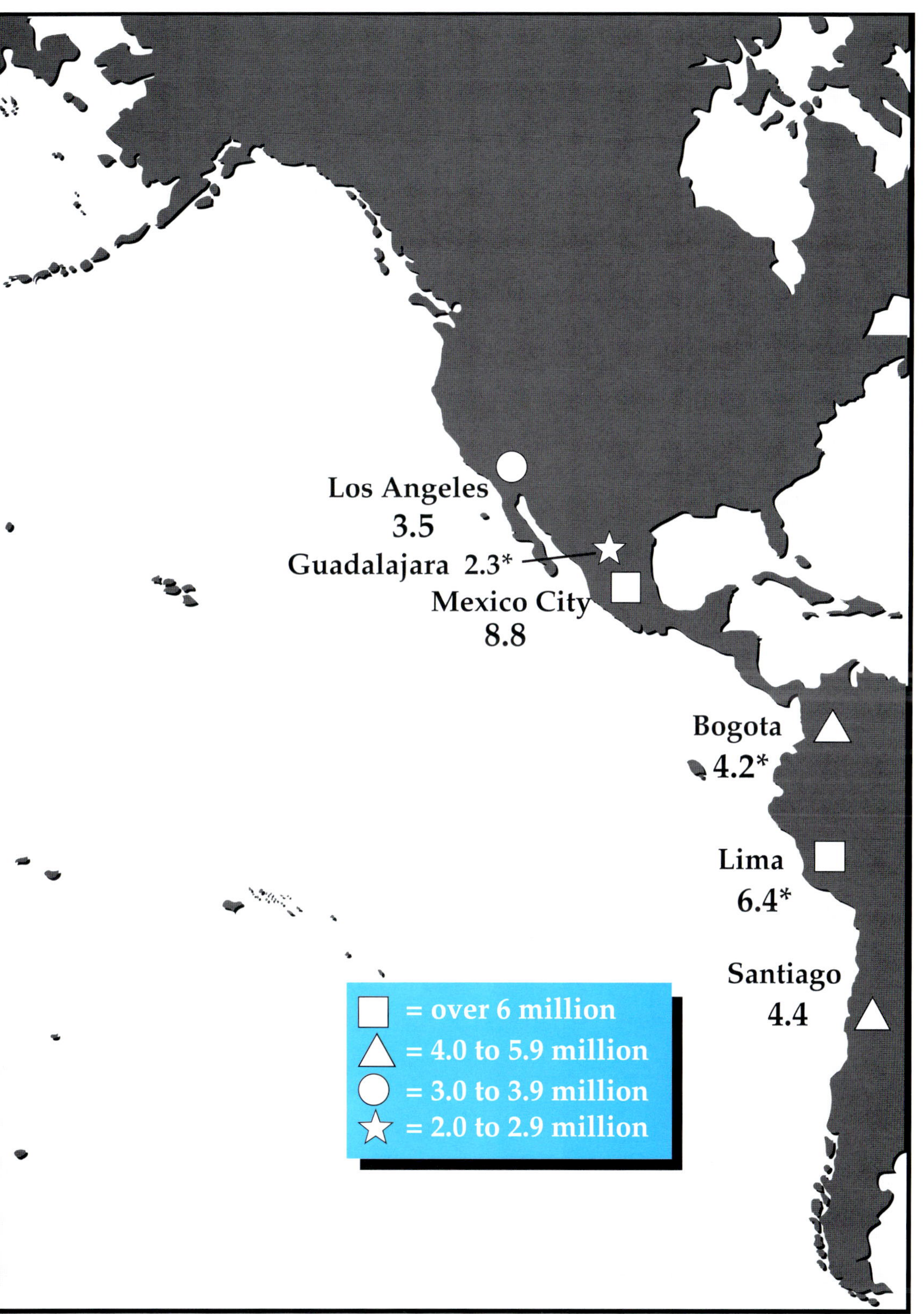

Los Angeles
3.5
Guadalajara 2.3*
Mexico City
8.8
Bogota
4.2*
Lima
6.4*
Santiago
4.4
= over 6 million
= 4.0 to 5.9 million
= 3.0 to 3.9 million
= 2.0 to 2.9 million

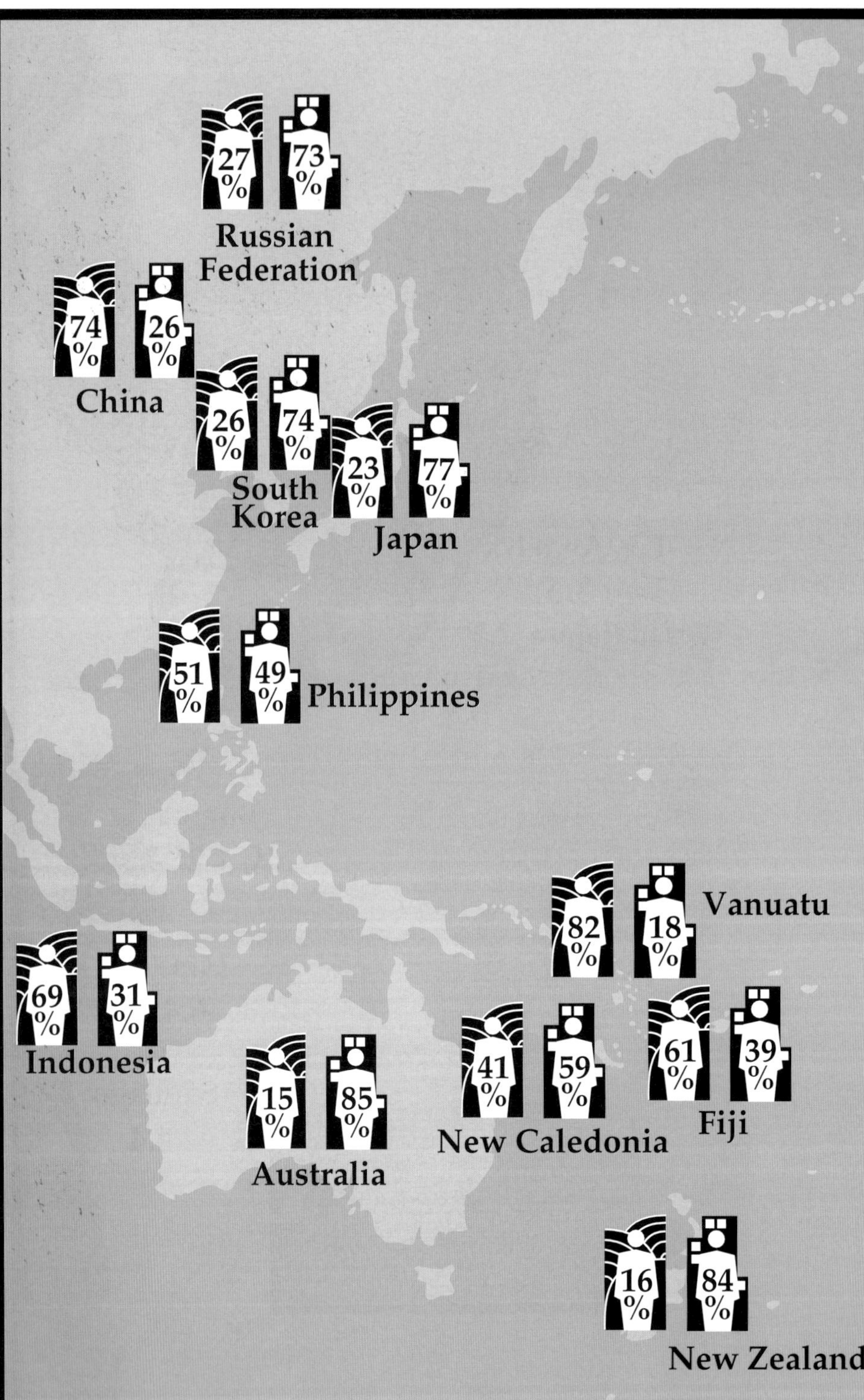

27%
73%
Russian Federation
74%
26%
China
26%
74%
South Korea
23%
77%
Japan
51%
49%
Philippines
82%
18%
Vanuatu
69%
31%
Indonesia
15%
85%
Australia
41%
59%
New Caledonia
61%
39%
Fiji
16%
84%
New Zealand

27%
73%
Canada
25%
75%
United States
56%
44%
Central America*
Colombia
33%
67%
Ecuador
43%
57%
Peru
30%
70%
15%
85%
Chile
Rural Urban
* = excludes
Belize and
San Salvador

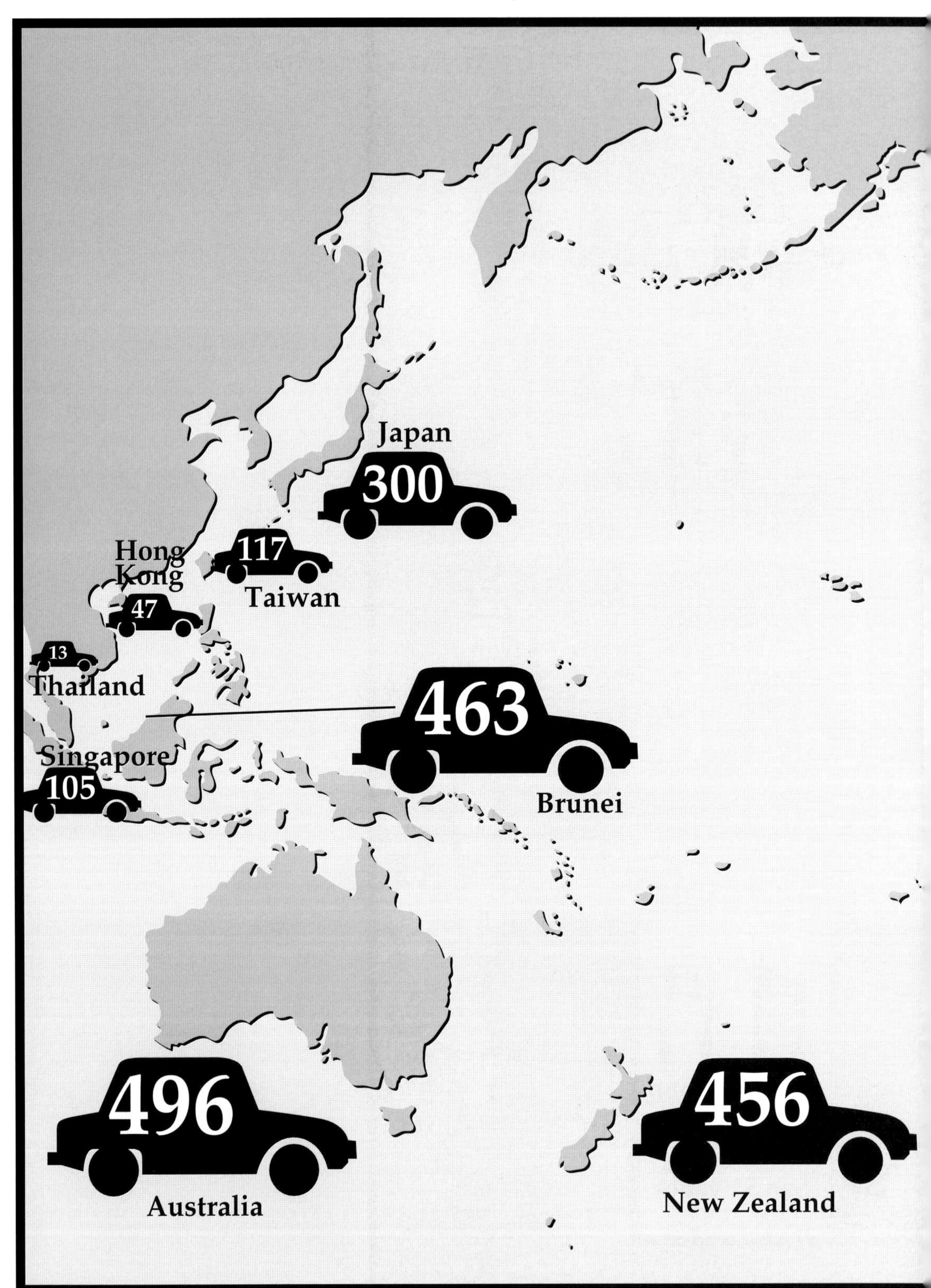

Japan
300
117
Taiwan
Hong Kong
47
13
Thailand
Singapore
105
463
Brunei
496
Australia
456
New Zealand

Passenger cars for every 1000 people, 1992

444
Canada
United States
577
66
Mexico
Costa
Rica
68
120
Colombia
55
Chile

Per capita gross national product
around the Pacific, 1992

Russian Federation
China
Japan
South
Korea
Hong
Kong
Philippines
Thailand
Papua New
Guinea
Solomon
Islands
Indonesia
Malaysia
Vanuatu
Singapore
Australia
New Zealand

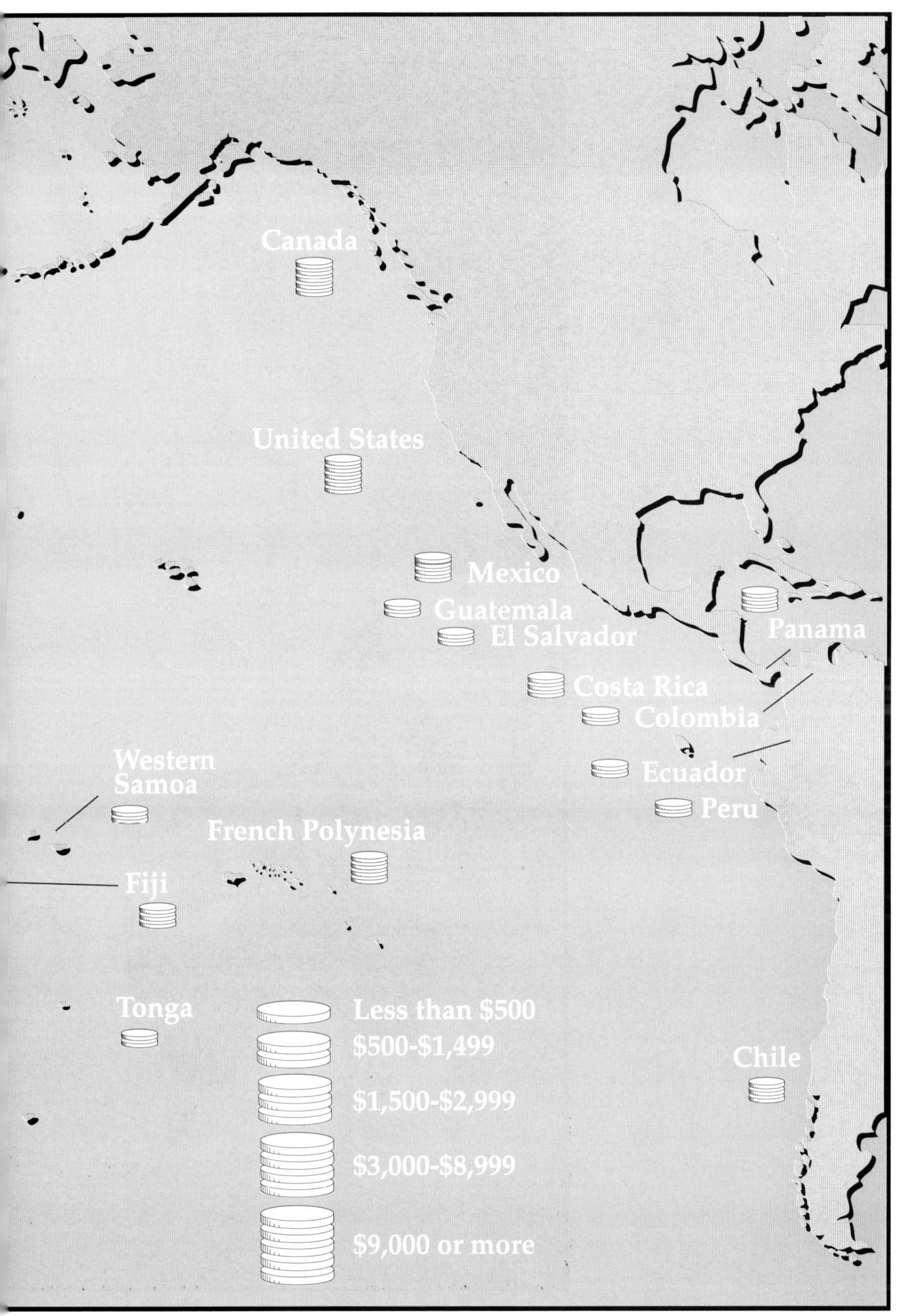

Canada
United States
Mexico
Guatemala
El Salvador
Panama
Costa Rica
Colombia
Ecuador
Peru
Western Samoa
French Polynesia
Fiji
Tonga
Chile
Less than $500
$500-$1,499
$1,500-$2,999
$3,000-$8,999
$9,000 or more

Ships cleared to leave port, in metric tons, 1991

317 mill
South Korea
402 mill
Japan
140 mill
20 mill
Philippines
Hong Kong
95 mill
Malaysia
Fiji
3 mill
Australia
76.5 mill
32 mill
New Zealand

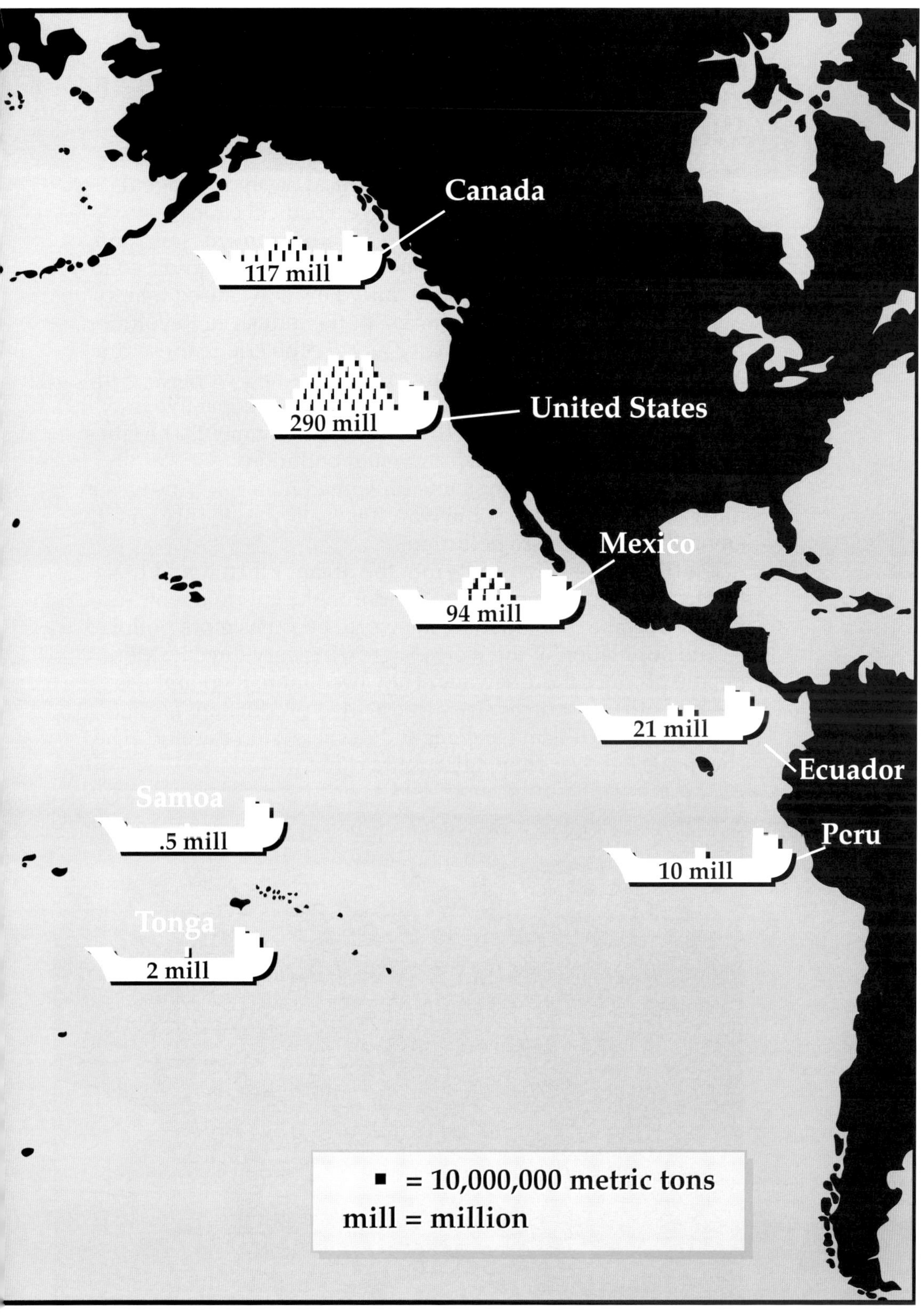

Canada
117 mill
United States
290 mill
Mexico
94 mill
21 mill
Ecuador
Samoa
.5 mill
Pcru
10 mill
Tonga
2 mill
= 10,000,000 metric tons
mill = million

Pollution

What Is Pollution?

Pollution occurs when chemical or physical agents (pollutants) that may have a bad effect on living things are released into the environment—air, land, or water. These pollutants may be gases, liquids, solids, or noise. Pollution is fairly new and caused mainly by human beings. Until the beginning of the Industrial Revolution, pollution had never been a major world problem. In those pre-industrial days, most people lived on farms and worked "with" the environment. Today a high percentage of people live in industrial cities, away from the natural environment. The cities are the source of much environmental pollution.

Most factories produce some unwanted material. This waste must be disposed of in some way. If it is allowed to mix with the environment, it causes pollution.

Oil from ships often spills into the ocean. When liquid fuels burn, poisonous fumes are released into the environment. As people become more mobile, the world becomes more polluted.

The population of the world is growing very quickly. More people produce more sewage. They need more food and use more of other resources. To increase food production, farmers spread more artificial fertilizer and pesticides on the land. The chemicals left over from agriculture cause pollution.

Rubbish dump in the coastal zone beside a stand of rare native palms. Packaging creates waste and leads to pollution. Seagulls are scavengers and find food in such places. Birds that need clean, fresh food cannot find it here.

We are all consumers. The things we consume are packaged in plastics and other disposable materials. This causes waste and often leads to pollution.

Most of the waste in the world ends up in the sea. Effluents from factories, farms, and homes is dumped first into drains. From there it flows—often untreated—into streams and rivers. The final step to the sea may take hours or months, but our waste finally spews out into the ocean—about 20 billion metric tons of it a year. Much of it remains for years in coastal waters. An estimated 90 percent never reaches deep water. Instead it stays close to shore where it interferes with the most productive breeding grounds of fish and pollutes even the fairest beaches.

For these reasons, the deep oceans are not thought to be seriously polluted—even though materials such as radioactive rubbish and toxic wastes are deliberately released into the sea or burned in midocean. All the coastal areas in the world, by contrast, are already seriously polluted, from the Indian Ocean to the Atlantic, the Pacific to the Antarctic, and all the seas between.

More than two-thirds of the population of the world lives within 80 kilometers of a coast, and nearly half of its major cities are built on or near an estuary. These are some of the reasons coastal areas have become so badly polluted. They are also among the reasons it matters so much: those who depend on the sea inevitably suffer when its quality deteriorates.

For fishers, things are particularly serious. Most of the 20,000 varieties of fish and 30,000 types of mollusks in the world come

Boom system for cleaning up oil spills on beaches. Victoria, Australia.

from coastal waters. Of the
world fish catch, 90 percent is
taken near the shore. Pollution
is threatening that catch, which
provides much of the animal
protein eaten by humans.
Sludge from sewers has ruined
many of the best shellfish beds
in the United States, and in
1969 it was estimated that 70
percent of the fish kills on the
shores of that country were
caused by either industrial
waste or agricultural runoff
that had been discharged into
the sea.

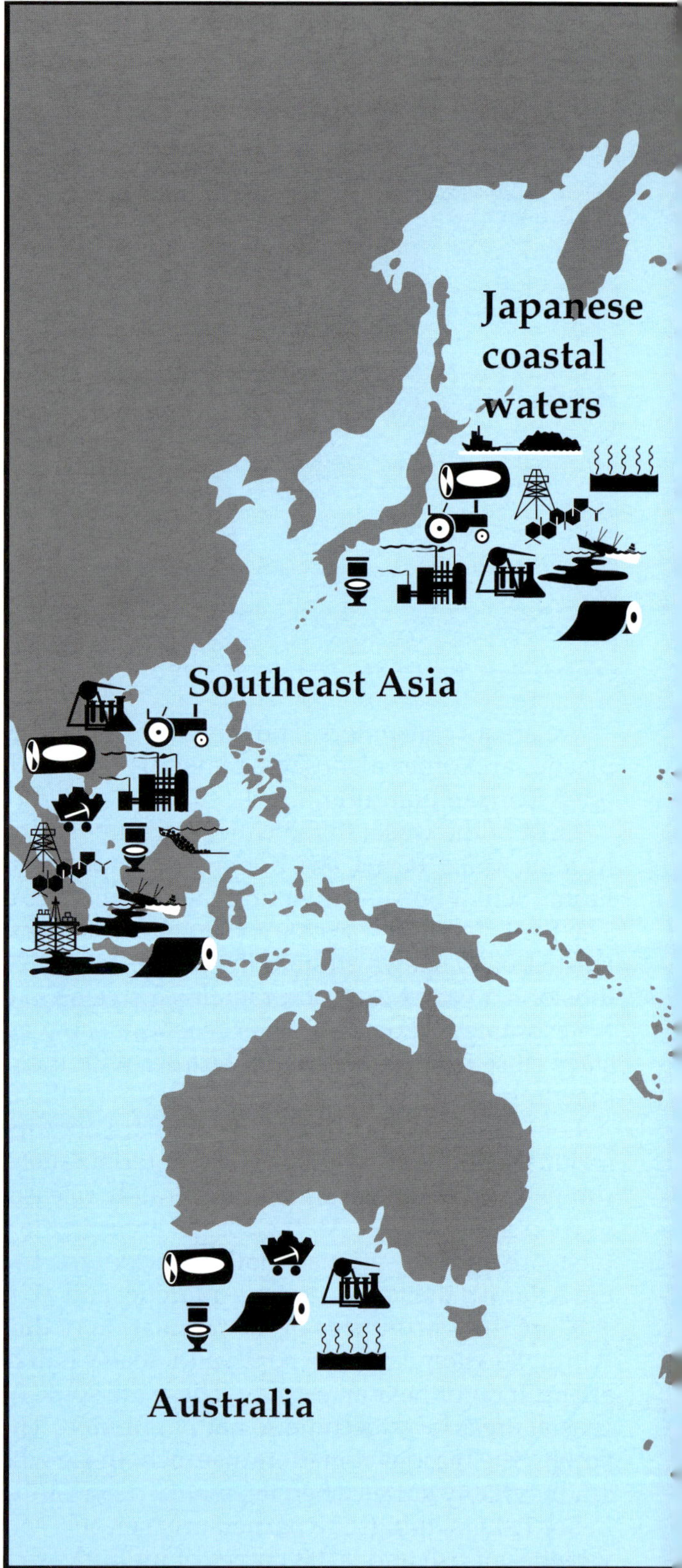

How the seas are polluted

North America
Southeast Pacific
New Zealand
Sewage
Petroleum
Petroleum
Petroleum
Mining
Radioactive
Food and beverage
Metal
Chemical
Pulp and
Agricultural
Siltation
Thermal
Dumping sewage and

The Pathways of Pollution

The technology that has made life more comfortable for the human race has huge costs. For example, poisonous chemicals poured into rivers are carried to the sea. Plants and animals living in both the rivers and the ocean are affected. Land animals that drink the river water also take in poisons. Water soaks into the ground where it affects the plants and eventually the ocean plants and animals. From the land, it flows with water to the sea, and when the rocks of the seabed break up into sand and wash up on the beach, it affects the land again. Sometimes, people dump the material on the seabed or bury it deep in the rocks, but these rocks eventually break down.

Industrial Pollution

In southern Japan, facing the Pacific, sits a beautiful bay whose name means "Protected Waters." On a sunny day, if you look down from the mountain, you see a little fishing village nestled beside the bay. It seems an ideal place for people to live.

One day in 1958, the shallow water near the beach was suddenly full of dying fish. The excited children of the village ran down to the beach and gathered up lots of fish to take home to their mothers for dinner that night. The whole village had a feast.

The name of the bay is Minamata. The fish had died because they had been poisoned with mercury released into the bay by a factory nearby. Mercury attacks and destroys the central nervous system. When you have had too much of it, you lose control of your arms and legs. Your whole body twitches because the nerves that carry the messages from your brain to your limbs and all over the body are destroyed and the messages that get through are garbled.

The mercury poisoning at Minamata had been going on for years. The whole village was poisoned. In the early 1970s the people of the village took the company to court and won.

This is probably one of the clearest cases in the world of poisoning by industrial pollution. It helped to change the way people around the world thought about pollution. Many had been willing to put up with it for the sake of the prosperity brought by industrial development. Now, however, few people who understand what happened at Minamata would be willing to make such a trade-off.

Since the Minamata case, both governments and industry have been much more concerned about mercury.

There are of course many other pollutants that get into our water, both freshwater and seawater. Some of the worst of them are shown in the following chart.

WHAT IT IS	WHAT IT HURTS	WHAT IT DOES
Mercury		In humans, harms the nervous system and causes paralysis and abnormalities in babies.
Cadmium		In humans, leads to emphysema, liver and kidney damage, and "Itai-itai byo" (ouch ouch disease)–a very painful affliction that deforms bones.
Lead		In humans, impairs mental health and increases the chance of stillbirth and miscarriage.
Raw sewage		Causes illness in people and smothers plants and animals.
Oil		Kills plants and animals.
Nitrogen oxides		Cause water plants to grow so much that aquatic animals die.*
Phosphorous oxides		Cause water plants to grow so much that aquatic animals die.*
Agricultural		Build up in aquatic animals and plants, and poison other animals farther up the food chain. These animals die.
Heat		Hot water flowing into rivers kills some aquatic plants and animals. Others that like warmer water live there and the environment changes.*
Acid rain		Factories release gases into the air that combine with rainwater to form acid. Acid kills plants and aquatic animals.*
Garbage		Ships and some countries dump their garbage in the sea, where it floats. Aquatic animals become entangled and suffocate in it.

*The pollutant has a secondary effect on marine mammals: the health of marine mammals depends on the purity and availability of their food.

SYMBOLS

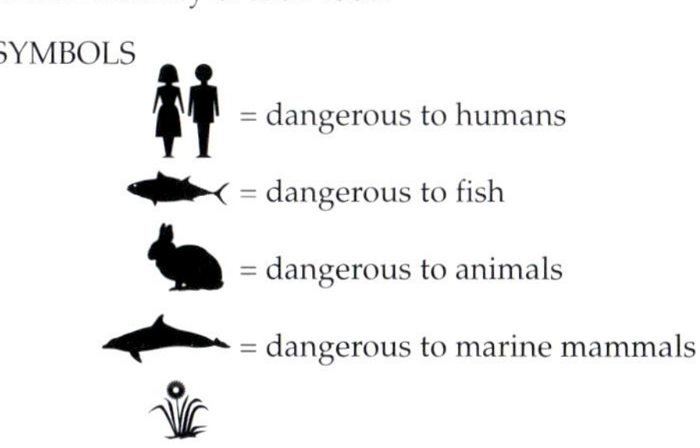

Pollutants in our water

Solid Waste

Waste disposal is becoming an ever greater problem. People demand more products and, increasingly, these products are designed to be disposable. Advertising and marketing people know that consumers like interesting packages, and so more and more products are brightly packaged to help them sell. This packaging creates more waste.

Waste Recycling

Some cities have recycling plants to recycle their waste. Unfortunately it is often cheaper to make new materials than to recycle old products. There are also many materials that cannot be recycled with today's technology.

Dumping of Waste

Waste from towns and cities is often dumped in the coastal zone, either directly into the sea or into the rivers where it may be carried to the sea. Solid waste may be used to reclaim land from the sea or to fill in valleys or holes. Waste dumps are unsightly and cause pollution. On small Pacific islands waste can be a major problem.

Carbon Dioxide

Ninety-five percent of the carbon dioxide (CO_2) generated by the human race is produced in the northern hemisphere. The atmospheres of the northern and southern hemispheres do not mix very well, so most of it stays there.

Sewage

Sewage is human waste from toilets, and water from baths and showers, kitchens, and laundries. In some places it includes industrial waste. Sewage contains many bacteria that came from human bodies and are dangerous to human beings. They can cause everything from slight stomach upsets to death from cholera.

In some places, the problem of what to do with raw sewage is solved by pouring the sewage into rivers or into the sea. Here it is diluted and carried away. Unfortunately, it is not carried far enough away and not diluted enough. What is more, the rivers and the sea are polluted by the sewage, and their ecosystem can be destroyed.

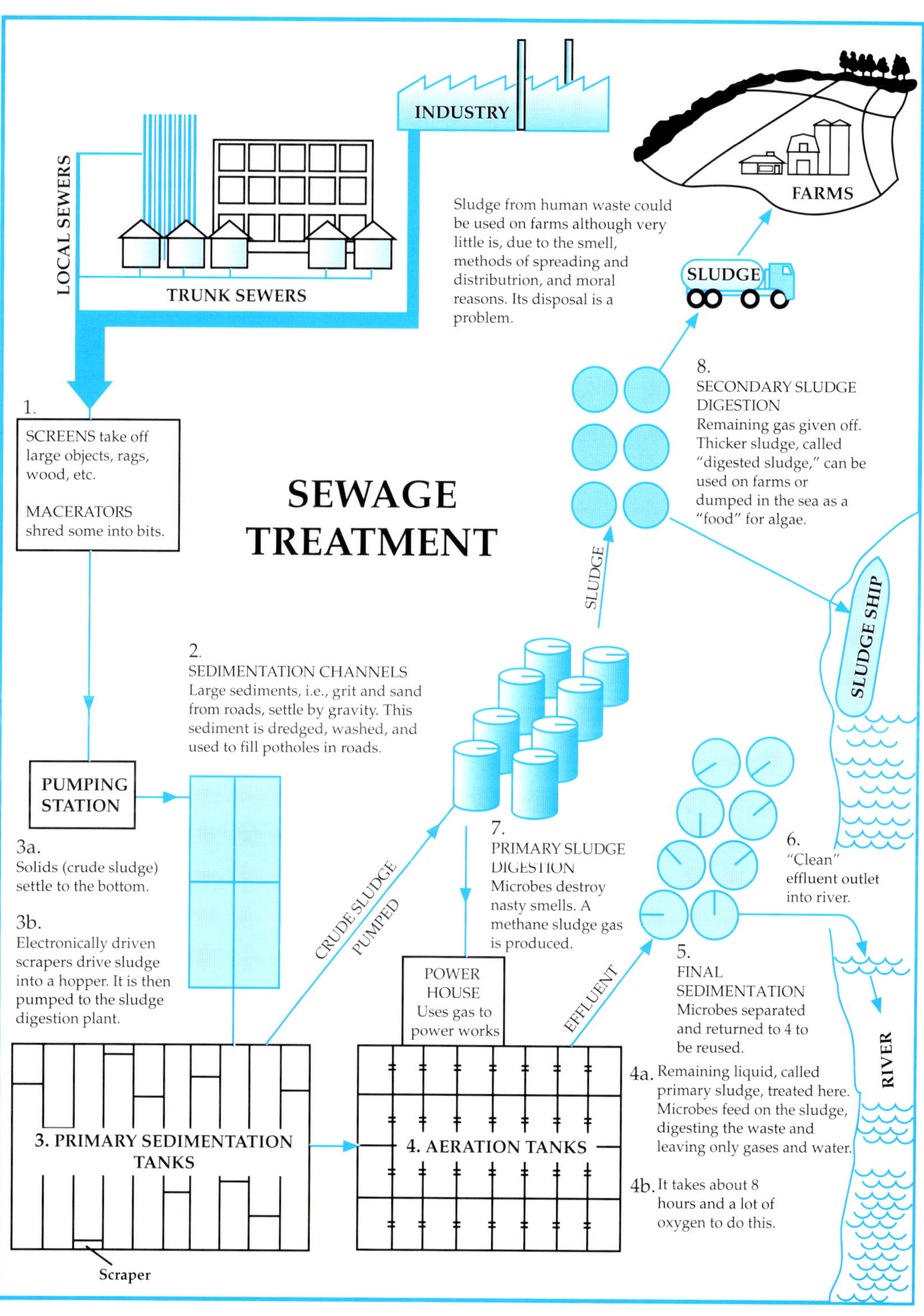

LOCAL SEWERS
TRUNK SEWERS
INDUSTRY
FARMS
SLUDGE
SEWAGE TREATMENT
Sludge from human waste could be used on farms although very little is, due to the smell, methods of spreading and distribution, and moral reasons. Its disposal is a problem.
1.
SCREENS take off large objects, rags, wood, etc.
MACERATORS shred some into bits.
2.
SEDIMENTATION CHANNELS
Large sediments, i.e., grit and sand from roads, settle by gravity. This sediment is dredged, washed, and used to fill potholes in roads.
PUMPING STATION
3a.
Solids (crude sludge) settle to the bottom.
3b.
Electronically driven scrapers drive sludge into a hopper. It is then pumped to the sludge digestion plant.
3. PRIMARY SEDIMENTATION TANKS
Scraper
CRUDE SLUDGE PUMPED
POWER HOUSE
Uses gas to power works
4. AERATION TANKS
7.
PRIMARY SLUDGE DIGESTION
Microbes destroy nasty smells. A methane sludge gas is produced.
8.
SECONDARY SLUDGE DIGESTION
Remaining gas given off. Thicker sludge, called "digested sludge," can be used on farms or dumped in the sea as a "food" for algae.
SLUDGE
SLUDGE SHIP
EFFLUENT
5.
FINAL SEDIMENTATION
Microbes separated and returned to 4 to be reused.
4a. Remaining liquid, called primary sludge, treated here. Microbes feed on the sludge, digesting the waste and leaving only gases and water.
4b. It takes about 8 hours and a lot of oxygen to do this.
6.
"Clean" effluent outlet into river.
RIVER

In many places these days, sewage treatment plants filter the sewage and separate the water from the solid matter. The solid matter, called sludge, can be burned, buried, or made into fertilizer. Even so, some waste gets into rivers and the sea.

Sewage can be a dangerous pollutant when it is put in the wrong place or when the quantity is large. It damages the environment in a number of ways.

- When plant or animal matter decays, it uses up oxygen, and animals trying to live in the water die of suffocation. Sludge is decaying matter, and so it kills animals.

- When sewage has been treated, there is much less decaying matter. It does not use as much oxygen, but it still contains nitrates and phosphates. They are nutrients for plants. Thus, the water will be a much better place for plants to grow than it was before. This sounds good, but it isn't. Algae will grow much more easily than before and eventually the water may be covered in green slime. The slime blocks the light at the surface. Plants produce oxygen in the daytime and use it at night, and so at night animals in the water have a difficult time breathing.

Sign warns of a sewage spill on Sandy Beach, Oahu, Hawaii.

Fecal coliforms

Fecal coliforms are germs from human or animal waste. If the number in a river is very high, it is probably because the river contains a lot of sewage. Water with 100 fecal coliforms for every 100 milliliters of water is safe to drink. The Ganges River in India has been known to have as many as 7.3 million. This is caused by the sewage from 114 towns that flows into the river.

Nuclear Pollution

Ancient Greek philosophers decided that all things must be made up of tiny building blocks which are so small that nothing can be smaller. They called these units atoms. The philosophers were right, or very nearly right. In this century we have found that atoms are themselves made up of even tinier particles, held together by very powerful forces. Atoms can give off energy in the form of light, heat, and electricity when they combine in chemical reactions. The central nucleus of atoms such as uranium can be split to give many times the energy of a chemical reaction.

A kilogram of uranium will produce 2.5 million times more heat than can be produced by burning a kilogram of coal or oil. This heat energy can be used to produce electricity. Nuclear power plants save fossil fuel.

Unfortunately, nuclear reactions also produce waste that continues to give off harmful energy for thousands of years. This means that the waste from nuclear power stations has to be stored in very safe places. Although people have been producing nuclear waste since the 1930s, nobody has yet found a safe way to store it.

Nuclear explosions create clouds of poisonous radioactive dust, and the areas where they explode are dangerous to human beings and to plants and animals for many years afterwards. The human beings who eat the poisoned animals get a double dose of poison—from the air and from the food. Nations have been testing nuclear weapons since the 1940s. It is not surprising that they tend to choose places as far away from their own land and people as possible. The Pacific is enormous and the islands in it are small. The population of most of them is also small. Many nations have therefore thought it was a good idea to explode their test bombs or dump their nuclear waste in the Pacific, either on islands or in the sea.

The bombs that in 1945 devastated Hiroshima and Nagasaki and brought the Pacific war to an end were very small bombs. Those tested on the other islands of the Pacific were much more powerful. Nuclear weapons were tested on Bikini Atoll in the Marshall Islands between 1946 and 1958 (23 tests), and on Eniwetok Atoll nearby between 1948 and 1958 (43 tests). Both these areas are still unsafe for human beings. The people who used to live there have a choice: they can stay away from their island, or they can go back and risk damage to their health. Now only France tests nuclear weapons in the Pacific, even though New Zealand, Australia, and other Pacific nations have protested.

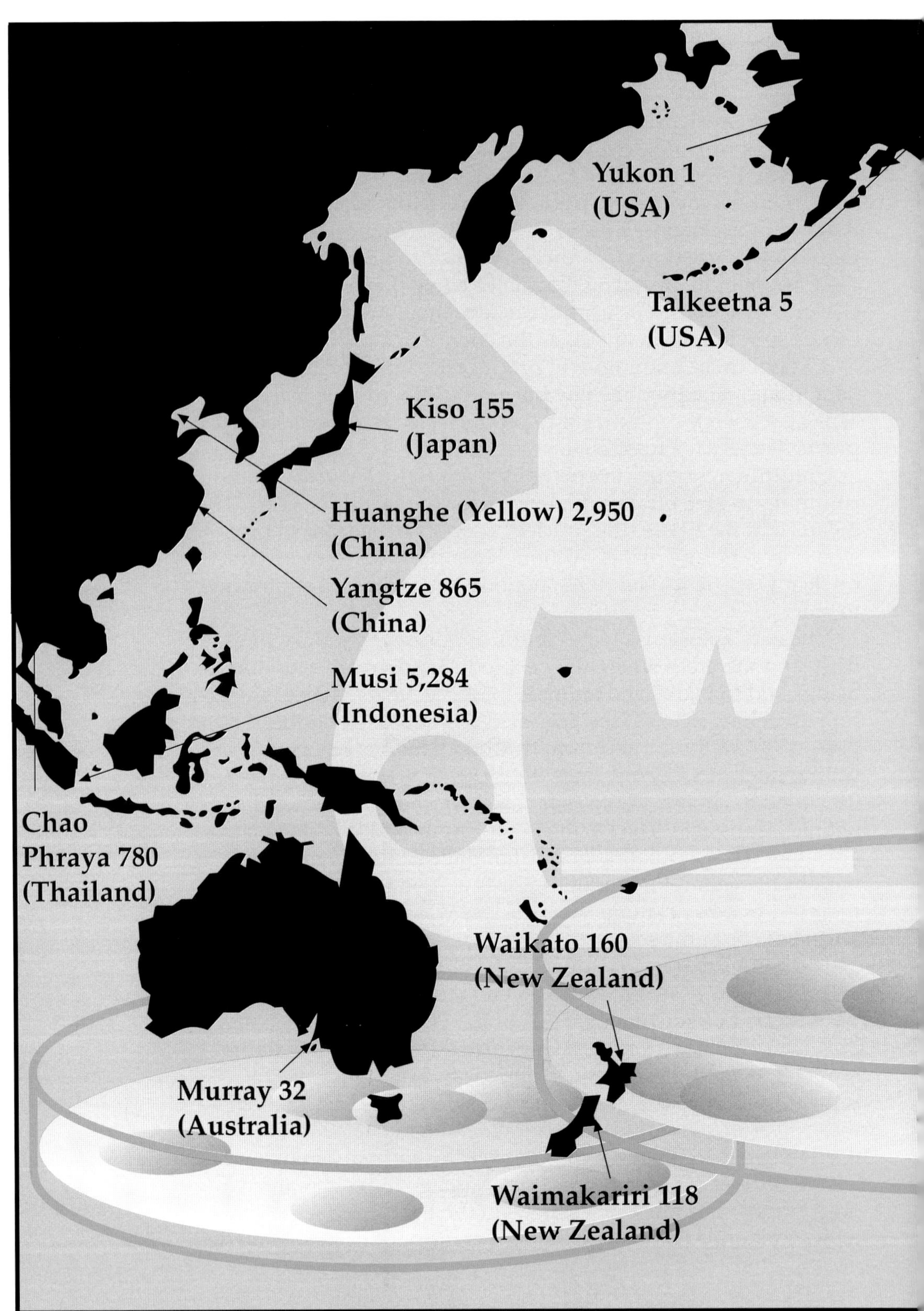

Yukon 1
(USA)
Talkeetna 5
(USA)
Kiso 155
(Japan)
Huanghe (Yellow) 2,950
(China)
Yangtze 865
(China)
Musi 5,284
(Indonesia)
Chao
Phraya 780
(Thailand)
Waikato 160
(New Zealand)
Murray 32
(Australia)
Waimakariri 118
(New Zealand)

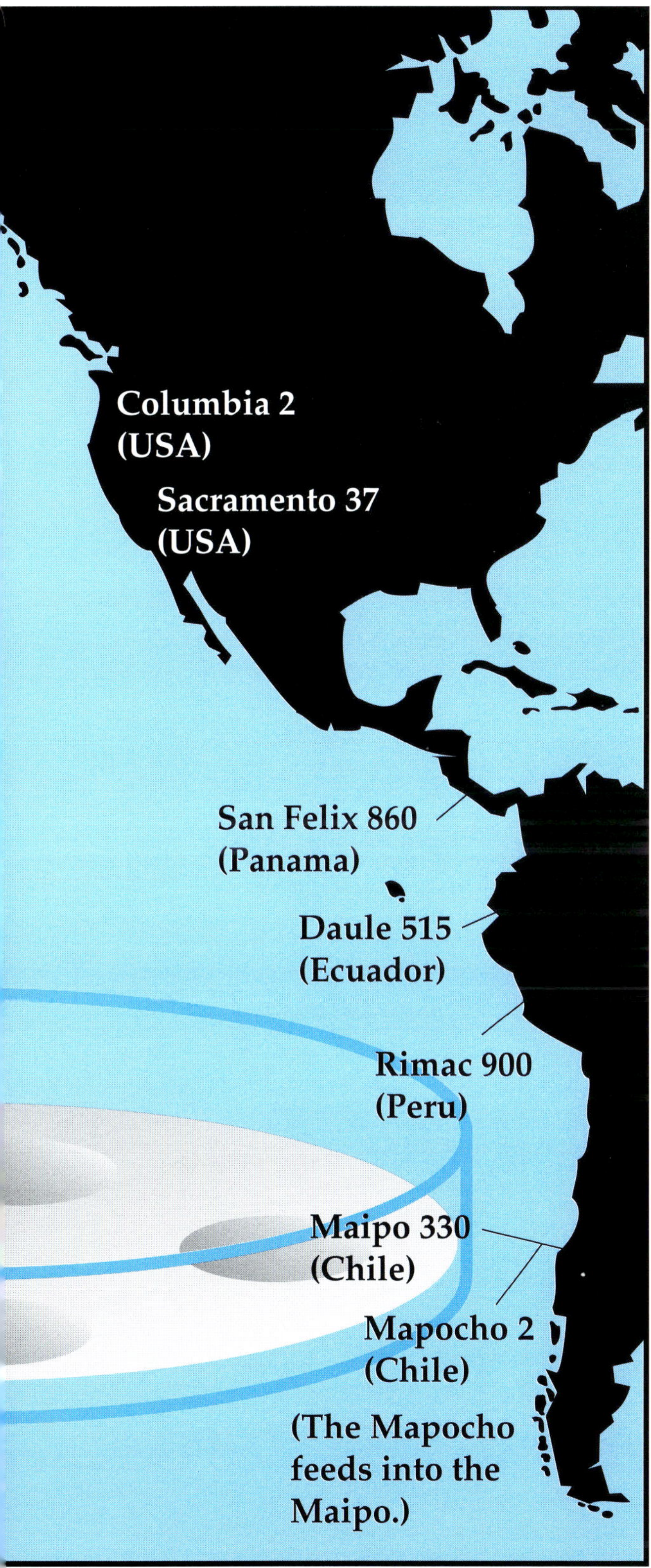

How clean are our rivers? The figures represent the number of fecal coliforms in a river for every 100 milliliters of water.

Nuclear power generated in and near the
Pacific, 1986.

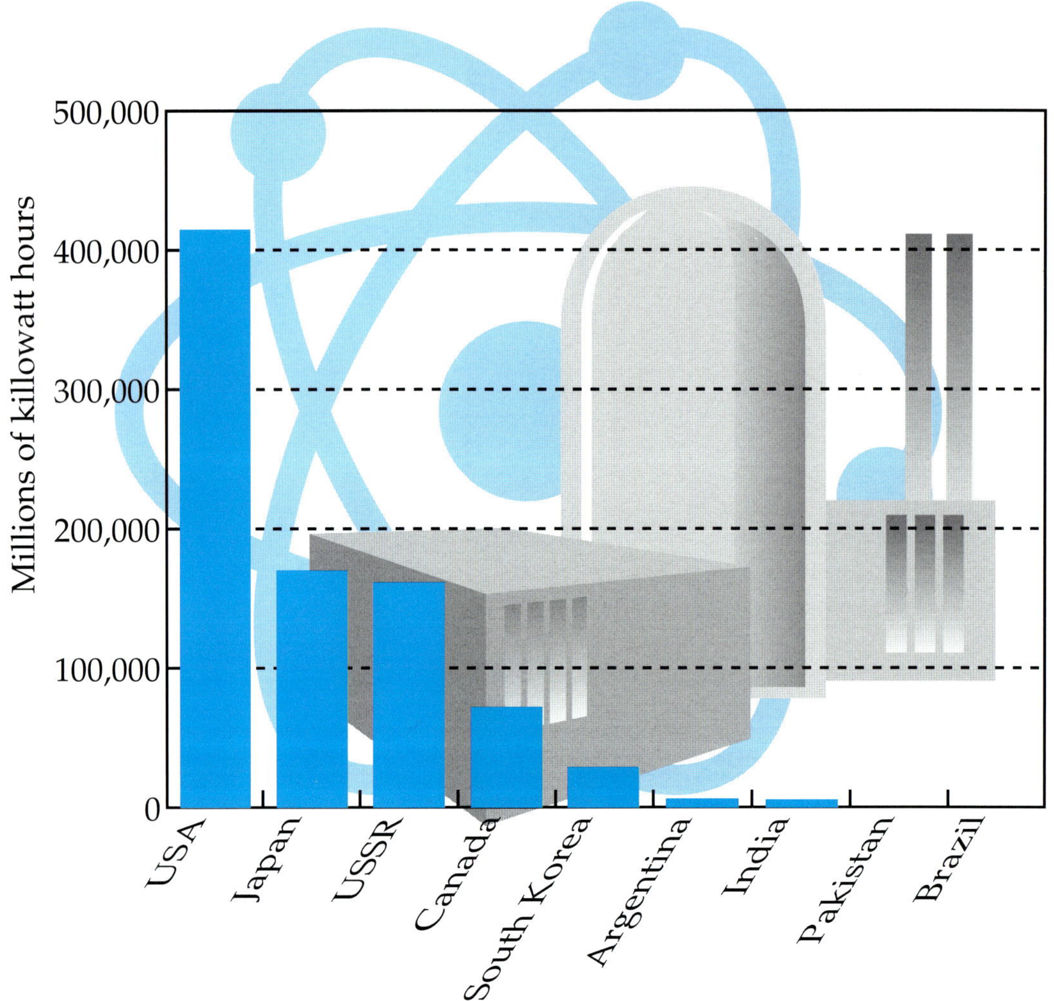

500,000
400,000
300,000
200,000
100,000
0
Millions of killowatt hours
USA
Japan
USSR
Canada
South Korea
Argentina
India
Pakistan
Brazil

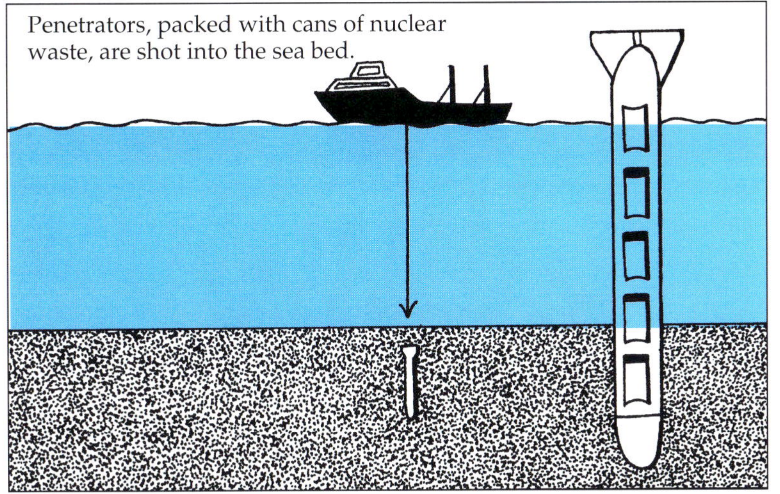

Penetrators, packed with cans of nuclear waste, are shot into the sea bed.

Proposed methods
for dumping
radioactive
materials at sea

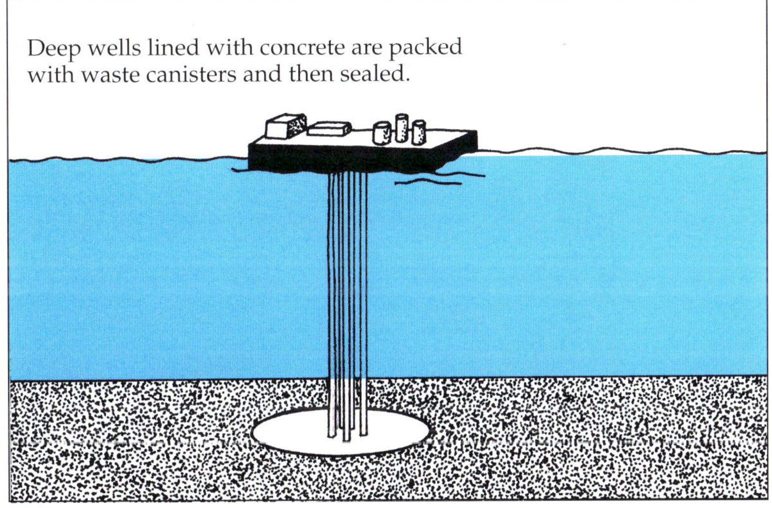

Deep wells lined with concrete are packed with waste canisters and then sealed.

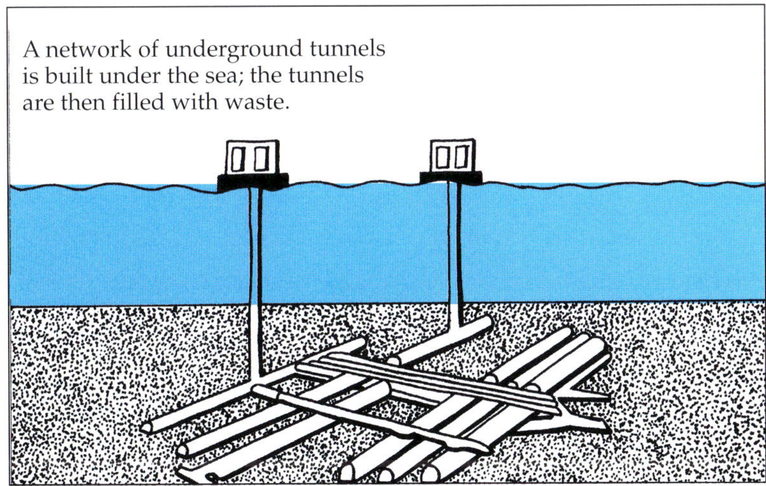

A network of underground tunnels is built under the sea; the tunnels are then filled with waste.

Nuclear power stations in the Pacific,
1991—operating and planned

Former USSR
China
Japan
South Korea
Taiwan

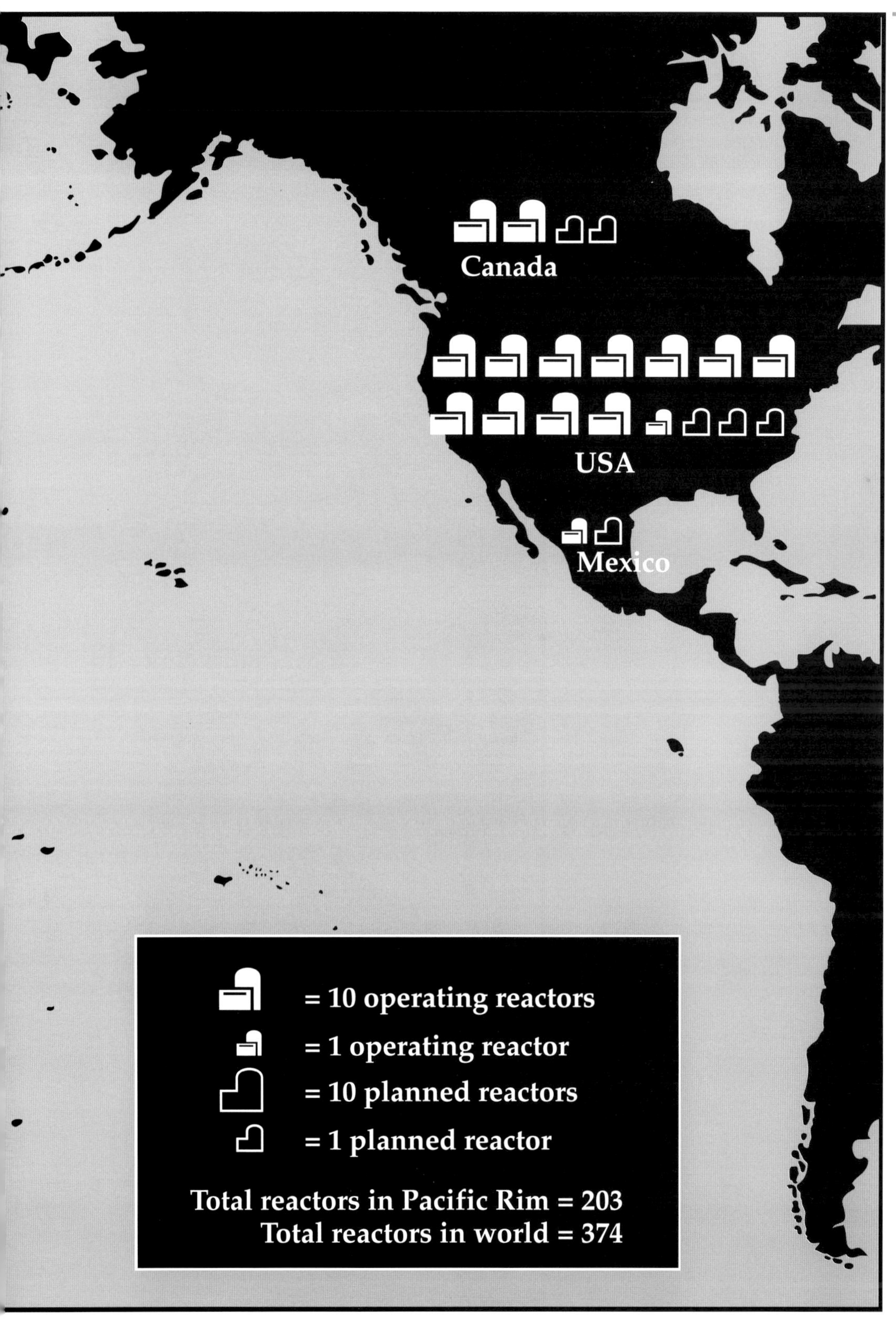

Canada
USA
Mexico
= 10 operating reactors
= 1 operating reactor
= 10 planned reactors
= 1 planned reactor
Total reactors in Pacific Rim = 203
Total reactors in world = 374

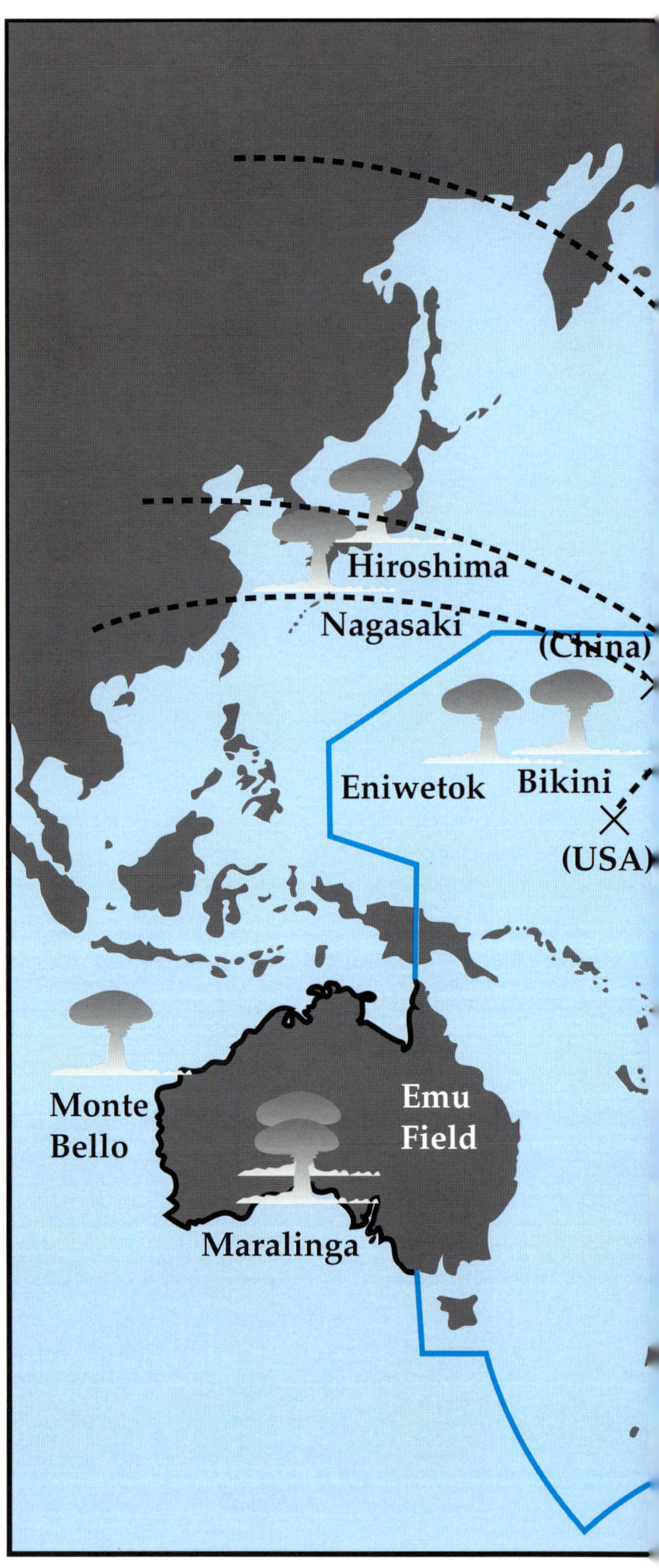

The nuclear Pacific, past and present. The U.S. dropped atomic bombs on Japan in WW II. The U.S. and Great Britain tested nuclear weapons until the early 1960s. In 1995 France resumed underground testing on Mururoa Atoll. American, Soviet, and Chinese missiles are fired to a variety of splashdown points in the Pacific. The outlined area represents the nuclear-free zone declared by a number of Pacific nations.

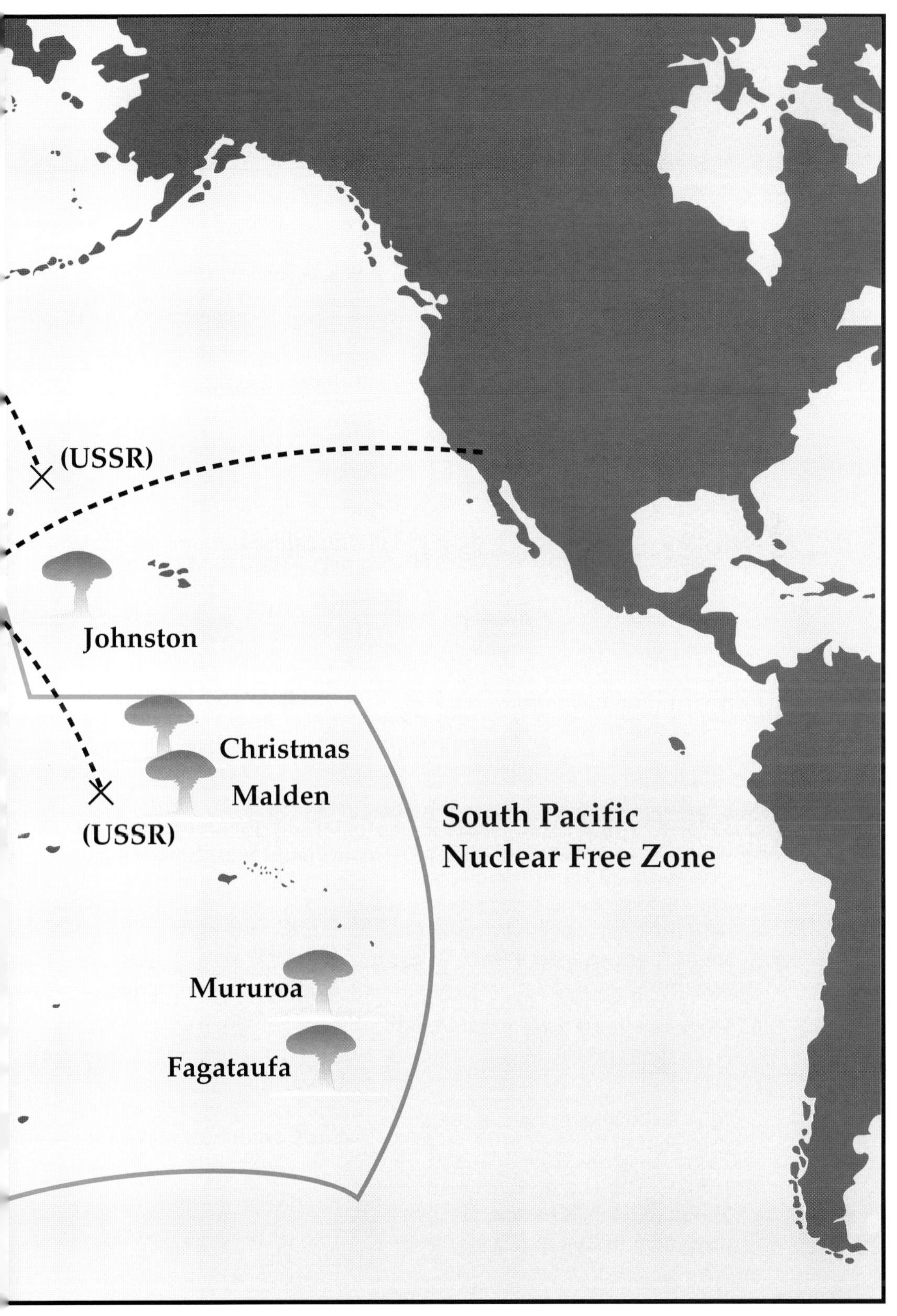
(USSR)
Johnston
Christmas
Malden
(USSR)
South Pacific
Nuclear Free Zone
Mururoa
Fagataufa

Nuclear Events Affecting the Pacific

1945. Atomic bombs were dropped on Hiroshima and Nagasaki.

1946. U.S. tested atomic bombs at Bikini atoll in the Marshall Islands which had recently been captured from Japan. Tests continued until 1958 (23 tests).

1948. U.S. tested at Eniwetok Atoll, also in the Marshall Islands. Testing finished in 1958 (43 tests).

1952. First hydrogen bomb was tested at Enewetak atoll.

1952. Britain tested nuclear weapons on the Monte Bello Islands in the Indian Ocean, and at Emu Field and Maralinga in the Australian desert. Testing ended in 1957 (12 tests).

1954. Several islands and a Japanese fishing boat were exposed to fallout from a U.S. test at Bikini atoll. Islanders, fishermen, and military personnel suffered radiation poisoning.

1956. Two more tests were carried out on the Monte Bello Islands.

1957. British testing in Australia ended.

1958. U.S. testing in the Marshall Islands ended. U.S. testing on Johnston Island began. It ended in 1962 (12 tests).

1962. Britain and the U.S. began a series of 25 tests on Christmas Island in the Pacific. U.S. testing on Johnston Island ended.

1965. A nuclear bomb fell overboard from an American aircraft carrier in Japanese waters. Some leakage has since been noted.

1966. French atmospheric tests began at Mururoa Atoll near Tahiti.

1973. Some Bikinians returned home, although they had been told it was not yet safe.

1973. Australia, New Zealand, and Fiji took France to the International Court of Justice to challenge French testing in the Pacific. France was asked to avoid nuclear tests that caused fallout in Australia and New Zealand. France announced that it did not accept that the court had the right to tell it what to do.

1974. France ended atmospheric testing.

1975. France began underground testing.

1975. UN supported the idea of a nuclear free zone for the Pacific. The First Nuclear Free Pacific Conference was held in Fiji.

1978. The Second Nuclear Free Pacific Conference was held in Ponape.

1978. Bikinians were evacuated because of high radiation levels.

1979. Nuclear accident at Mururoa. A bomb exploded on its way down the shaft, shattering the side of the atoll and causing local tidal waves.

1980. The French government said that it was testing a neutron bomb.

1981. Bikinians sought $450 million damages from U.S. government in a court case.

1982. People of Enewetak sought $500 million damages from the U.S. government in a court case.

1984. France bombed the *Rainbow Warrior.*

1986. New Zealand obtained $13 million compensation from France for the bombing of the *Rainbow Warrior.* A year later, Greenpeace obtained $8 million.

1986. Nuclear accident at a nuclear power station at Chernobyl in the USSR. Winds carried radioactive cloud over most of the northern hemisphere. Since the air of the northern and southern hemispheres does not mix very much, very little radioactive fallout, if any, reached the south Pacific, although Japan got more than Britain.

1986. Fourteen Pacific island nations plus Australia, France, New Zealand, Britain, and the United States concluded a United Nations convention for the protection of the natural resources and environment of the South Pacific region. This specified that they would not store nuclear waste in the 200-mile zones of 23 Pacific island countries and along the east coast of Australia.

1992. France, the U.S., Britain, and the USSR suspend underground testing.

1995. France resumes underground testing on Mururoa Atoll. Pacific nations respond with boycotts and protests.

The First Atomic Bombs

	Hiroshima	Nagasaki
Date and time of explosion	August 6, 1945, at 8:15 AM	August 9, 1945, at 11:02 AM
Size of the bomb—		
Length	3.0 meters	3.5 meters
Diameter	0.7 meters	1.5 meters
Weight	4.0 tons	4.5 tons
Power of the bomb	11.5–13.5 TNT	20–24 TNT
Buildings completely destroyed or burned (%)	62.9	22.7
Buildings half-destroyed, half-burned, and slightly damaged (%)	24.0	10.8
Number of human deaths (by the end of December 1945)	130,000–150,000	60,000–80,000

It is not only the people near the test islands who have problems. When the nuclear reactor at Chernobyl exploded in 1986, most of the northern hemisphere got an extra dose of radiation. Apart from accidents like this, it is probably true to say that these days, most of the harmful radiation we receive comes from X rays.

In the seven years between 1966 and 1972, Australian babies fed on cow's milk received an extra dose of radiation from the French nuclear tests. It was equal to about three years' extra natural radiation.

After the first British test in the Australian desert in 1952, the rainwater in Rockhampton was found to be 200 times as radioactive as it normally would be.

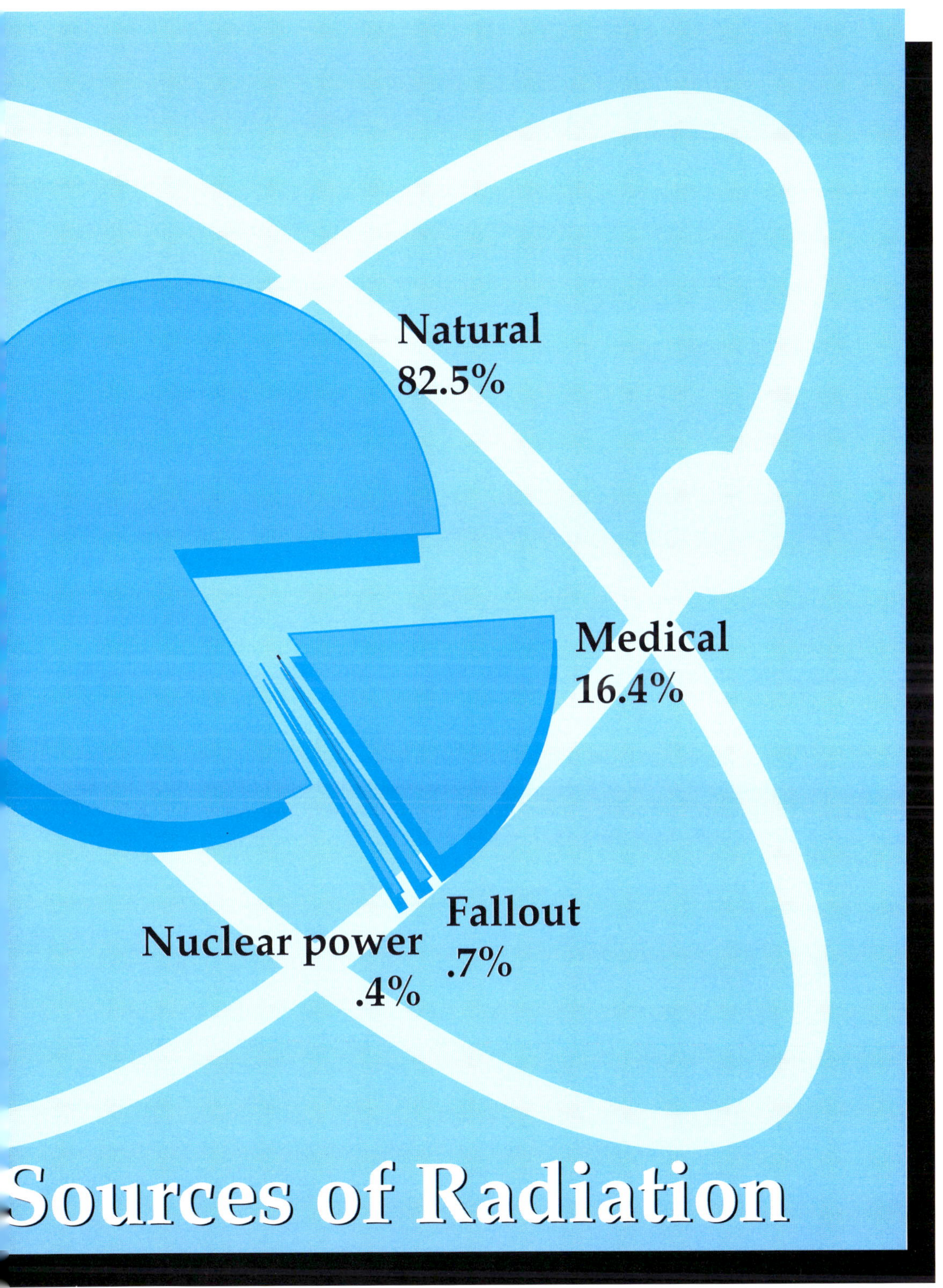

Sources of Radiation

The Question of Water

Freshwater and Salt Water

If you take a spade and dig deep enough, you may strike water. In some cases you may dig for a few seconds, in others you may have to drill hundreds of meters. In some places you may find no water at all. The water you find is generally very clean because it has been filtered through soil and rock. In areas where there are other minerals, the water may taste like those minerals. In areas where there are other metals in the soil, it may taste of those metals, but it will not have "dirt" in it.

Atoll well. On atolls, such as here in Kiribati, the limited amount of fresh water underground is easily contaminated or made salty by overuse.

Why is there water in the ground? Rain soaks down into the soil and then through underground rock. On volcanic islands some rock is very porous and the water soaks in extremely well. It is also perfectly filtered as it seeps through. In other places, water is trapped under hard rock and can flow underground for long distances. Seawater is denser than freshwater, so the weight of the seawater around the island stops the freshwater from pushing into the ocean. A lens-shaped body of freshwater thus forms under the island. This is called groundwater. If you drill here the water comes flowing up.

In the coastal zone, if you use too much groundwater, salt water from the sea flows in to take the place of the freshwater.

Problems of Increased Runoff

When you hose the garden, the water is absorbed by the soil almost immediately. If you hose asphalt or concrete, the water will form a puddle if the surface is flat and a stream if it slopes. In the 1890s, cities were small, streets often were not paved, and in the country and the city, rainwater absorbed into the soil. Only a part of it flowed into drains and rivers and went immediately to the sea.

In the 1990s cities are very large and extensively paved. Sometimes cities flood where no flooding ever occurred before because there is little soil to absorb the rainwater and it rushes in a torrent down the asphalt and concrete streets.

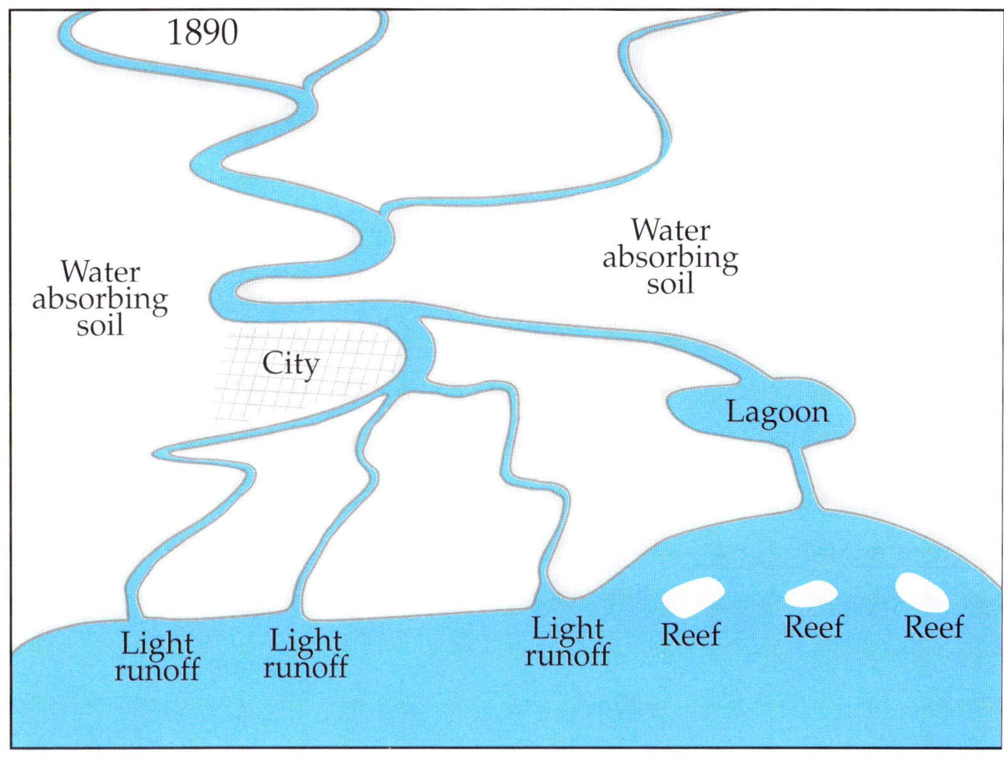

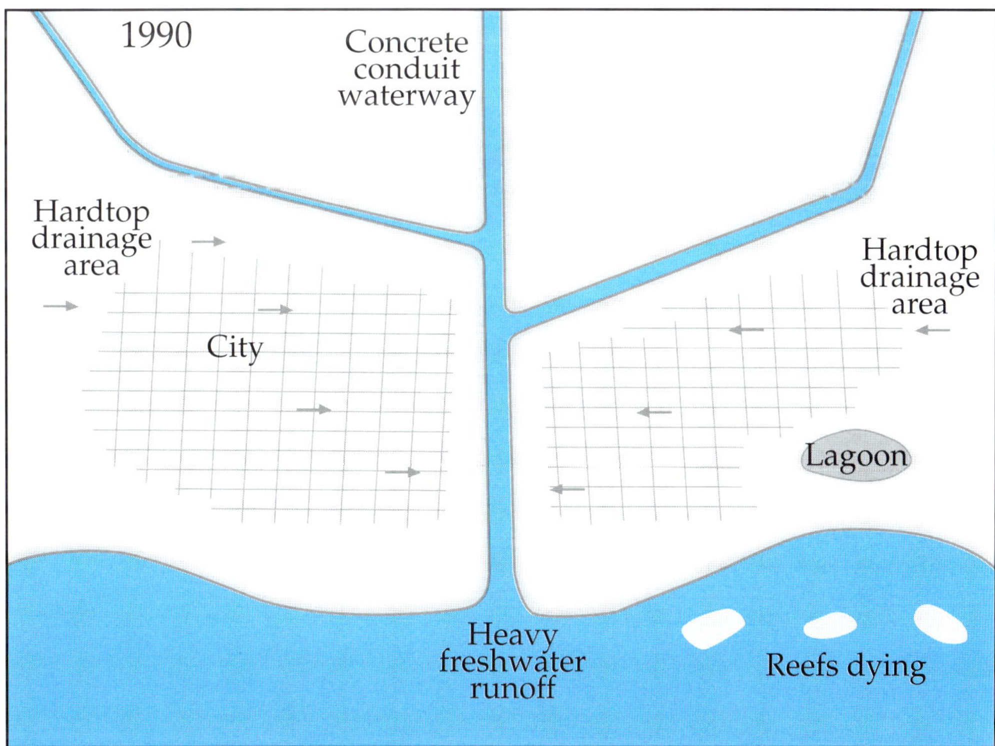

The effects of paving coastal areas

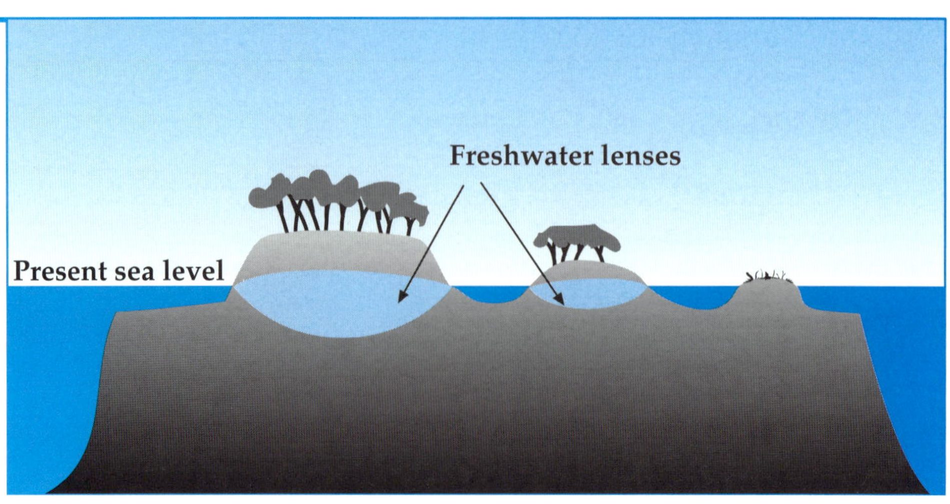

Freshwater lenses
Present sea level

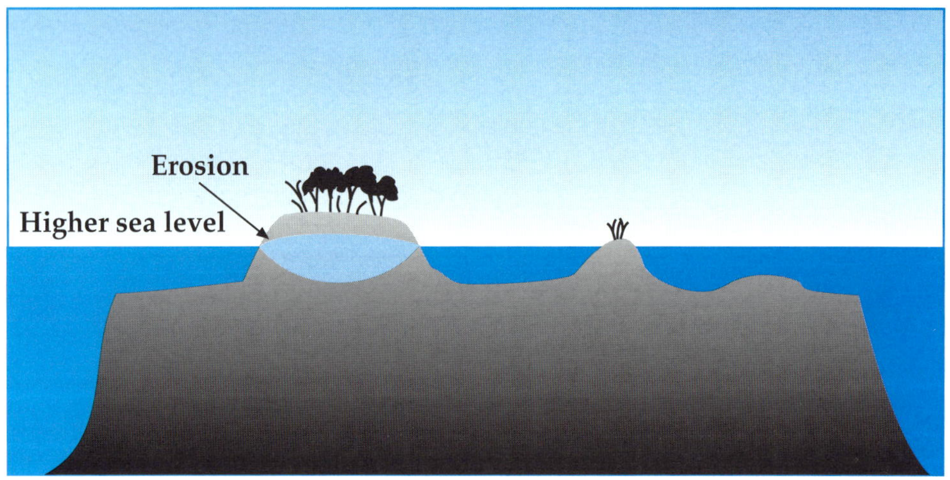

Erosion
Higher sea level

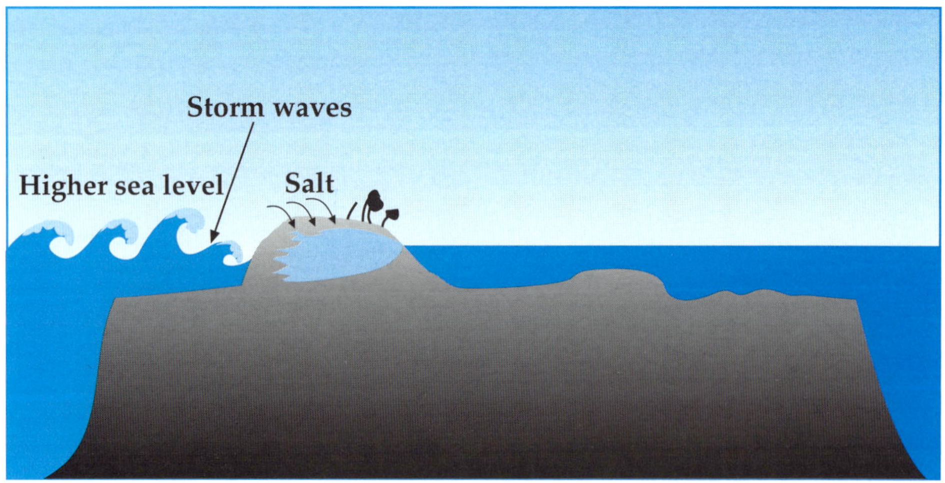

Storm waves
Higher sea level
Salt

In the 1890s many small streams carried the rainwater to the ocean, and along the way wetlands trapped it. The runoff from the land was light and distributed in various directions. In the 1990s many wetlands are gone, and small streams are channeled into one big river. Now there is a strong flow of freshwater out onto the coral reefs offshore.

Clean freshwater can be a pollutant too. It kills the living coral of reefs. Seawater has salt and other minerals dissolved in it and weighs more than the same volume of freshwater. The freshwater therefore floats on top of the seawater where it bathes the coral. Coral cannot live in freshwater. In the 1890s the layer of freshwater was thin and did not go far out into the sea. Now the layer is thick and it spreads over all the reefs. The reefs die.

Under many Pacific islands is a lens-shaped body of freshwater floating on top of and trapped by the seawater underneath. If the sea level rises, the level of the salt water under the island will rise too, leaving less space for freshwater. A one-meter rise in sea level could result in as much as a 30-meter reduction in the depth of the freshwater.

Many of the Pacific islands depend on groundwater for their water supply. In Hawaii, for example, there was barely enough groundwater in the 1980s for the population.

Uses of Water

Although water is vital for all life on earth, we tend to overlook its importance. What are the uses to which our water resources are put? The major categories are agricultural, industrial, and domestic. Very little of the water in the world is accessible for human use. In industrialized societies domestic water for bathing, washing, flushing toilets, and many other daily needs amounts to about 220 to 300 liters daily for each person.

Increasing urbanization and population growth have put great pressure on the available water in the heavily populated coastal zone. On small islands and coral atolls, freshwater may be in short supply. In large cities in the coastal zone it may be difficult to obtain clean freshwater, and so the water may have to be treated.

Many Pacific islands depend for their water supply on lens-shaped bodies of freshwater that float on the seawater underneath. When an island erodes, its lenses begin to shrink. In addition, salt water begins to seep into the lenses and pollute them.

Water is not an infinite resource, but we are fortunate that it is renewable. It is continuously recycled and cleaned by passing from the oceans to the atmosphere and back to the land, where it becomes available again for plants and animals, including human beings, that need freshwater.

The earth has 1400 million cubic kilometers of water.

Fifteen of the largest rivers in the world carry one-third of the runoff of the whole world. The Amazon River alone carries 15 percent.

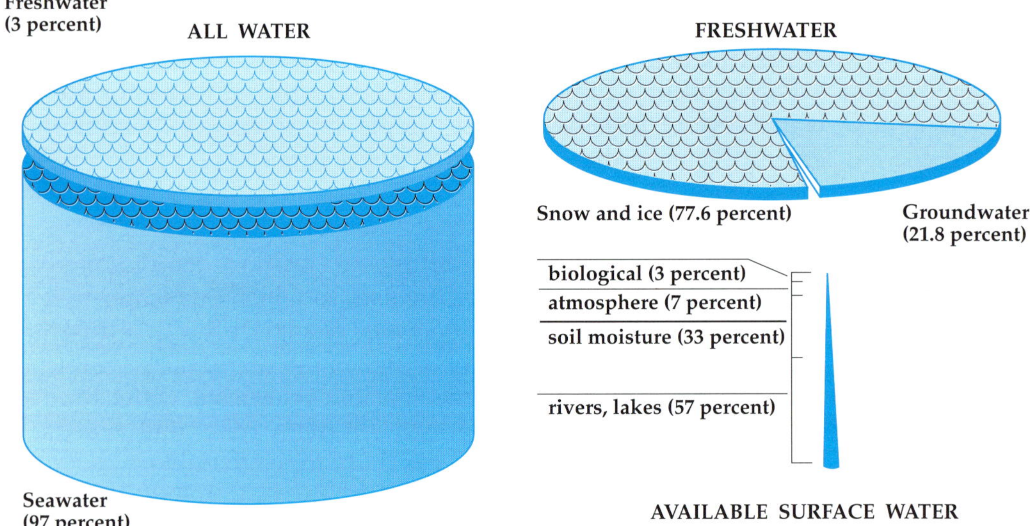

World water supply

Erosion

What is Natural Erosion?

The coast, as the collision point between the waves and the land, is a very active part of the surface of the earth. The contact zone is very narrow. It begins at the point at which waves first "feel" the land and extends to the top limit of storm waves at high tide. The energy collected by the waves over thousands of miles acts on this tiny strip of land, which is why it wears away so quickly. This wearing away is called erosion.

Most of the energy of the beach system comes from waves. With few exceptions, the changes in the beach result from waves crashing against the land. When the sea is set in motion, the moving water exerts stress against the coast and this may cause erosion.

Waves act as very efficient agents of erosion in a number of ways:

- Water crashes against rocks and cliffs, breaking them up.

- Pebbles and boulders caught in a wave dash against each other and break into smaller and smaller particles.

Spits should not be built on, and vegetation should be protected. Nestucca Spit, Oregon.

- Waves hurl boulders, pebbles, and sand against the base of a cliff or platform, undercutting the cliff.

Much of the material carried by wind and water is eventually dropped by the waves and forms beaches and spits. It should be remembered that coastal erosion is a continuous process and that it takes place over millions of years. A beach that appears to be stable may in fact be gradually eroding. Thus, the coastal zone is constantly changing.

Erosion has been going on since land first formed on the earth. Wind and water will erode rock. Soil and clay, so much softer than rock, erode even more quickly. Fire burns the trees, shrubs, and grasses that hold soil together. The soil blows away, leaving clay or rock. Waves erode the shore. These are the natural processes of erosion, but human beings have brought others.

Rain erosion. After a bulldozer made a path up a hill, heavy rains fell. The wet ground became soft and the tree fell down, taking large chunks of soil with it. Thus both the hill and the path were destroyed. Waimea Falls Park, Hawaii.

Wind erosion. The owners of this Oregon home built their house on a sand dune. The wind did the rest.

When Humans Intervene

Grazing animals crop the grass so closely that the topsoil blows away. The clay beneath is then carried off with rain and flood. When people cut down forests, the same thing happens. Elsewhere, they mine sand or gravel for construction and leave the earth gaping. They blast mountains open, looking for gold or iron, and wash the rock in rivers to separate out the metals. The soil and rocks are either carried away by the river, or they block it up. People use great hoses with enormous water pressure to wash away the rock. This is called hydraulic mining. Rivers are dammed, leaving the bed below the dam dry and open to erosion. Furthermore, dams can burst, and when they do, the rush

Mining activities can lead to erosion and the destruction of habitats. Goliath Gold Mine on the South Island of New Zealand.

Both rocks and wood have been used here to try to stop beach erosion, but they cannot withstand the power of the sea.

of water breaks up the soil and carries it down to the sea. To grow wheat or other European crops, farmers clear vast areas of forest. The now cultivated land, left exposed for part of the year, becomes sand. As a result, many places on the edge of deserts are turning into desert too.

Even in our own homes things go wrong. If we live near the beach and we water the garden too much, this will break up the clumps of soil. They can become sand and blow away or be carried away by water. If sand is dug up to put in foundations for buildings, it can blow away.

The steeper the slope, the greater the erosion. Therefore, mountains erode more easily than flat land. Volcanic islands are particularly in danger because volcanos are often steep.

The power of nature is enormous. When people change the coastline, they sometimes fail to allow for the impact of nature on what they have built. For example, developers built these houses in Pacific City, Oregon, on a cliff that was prone to erosion. When waves began to eat away at the cliff, the builders dumped large quantities of rocks in an attempt to stabilize the bank.

Now the same houses are threatened for a different reason: the rock provided a foothold for drifting sand, which is beginning to envelop the houses.

Many parts of continents rose millions of years ago out of the sea. Because the land was once seabed, there is now a layer of salt under the soil. If areas like this are then irrigated, the soil becomes wet and the water soaks down to the layer of salt. The salt dissolves in the water and soaks upwards so that now a layer of salt lies on the surface. Land that was once good for growing crops becomes useless desert.

When land is turned to desert, rainwater carries the sand down to the rivers, which in turn carry it to the sea. When the sand reaches the coast, it is dumped and the coast silts up. The land starts growing out into the sea. The Yellow River in China gets its name because it is really yellow. It is yellow from the volume of soil it carries from the dry lands through which it flows. The map shows how the coastline around the estuary of the Yellow River has changed over the centuries because of siltation.

In a river carrying a lot of silt into estuaries and bays, there is less light for the plants; in addition, the feeding and breathing systems of animals may become clogged with silt, so they may not survive so well.

The power of the sea is enormous. When people change the coastline, they sometimes fail to allow for the effect of the waves on what they have built. For example, during the Second World War, an army built a bridge halfway across the mouth of a river. The bridge altered the way the waves carried the sand into the estuary and onto the beach.

In the intervening years, the beach has silted up, so that where you could once step from a nice white beach into deep water and swim, you now have to walk hundreds of meters over mudflats before you find water deep enough for swimming. Also, the sea is eating away the cliffs so that the water is now within a couple of meters of the road, and on the other side of the road are houses. The government is dumping huge amounts of rock on the cliffs to stop them from being eaten away and to save the road and the houses.

In the Marlborough Sounds in New Zealand, logging has cleared the land of trees. This has exposed the soil, which has been washed down from the steep hills into the water of the sound, killing a variety of animals.

Tree roots help stop erosion. The roots of casuarinas are especially good for preventing erosion. It is no accident that they come from Australia, where erosion is particularly bad, or that they are now to be found on the beaches of many Pacific islands.

Rain
Fire
Vertical
farming
techniq
Roof runoff
Felling
Subsistence
farming

Wind
Land-clearing
techniques
Overgrazing
Hydraulic mining
Sluice

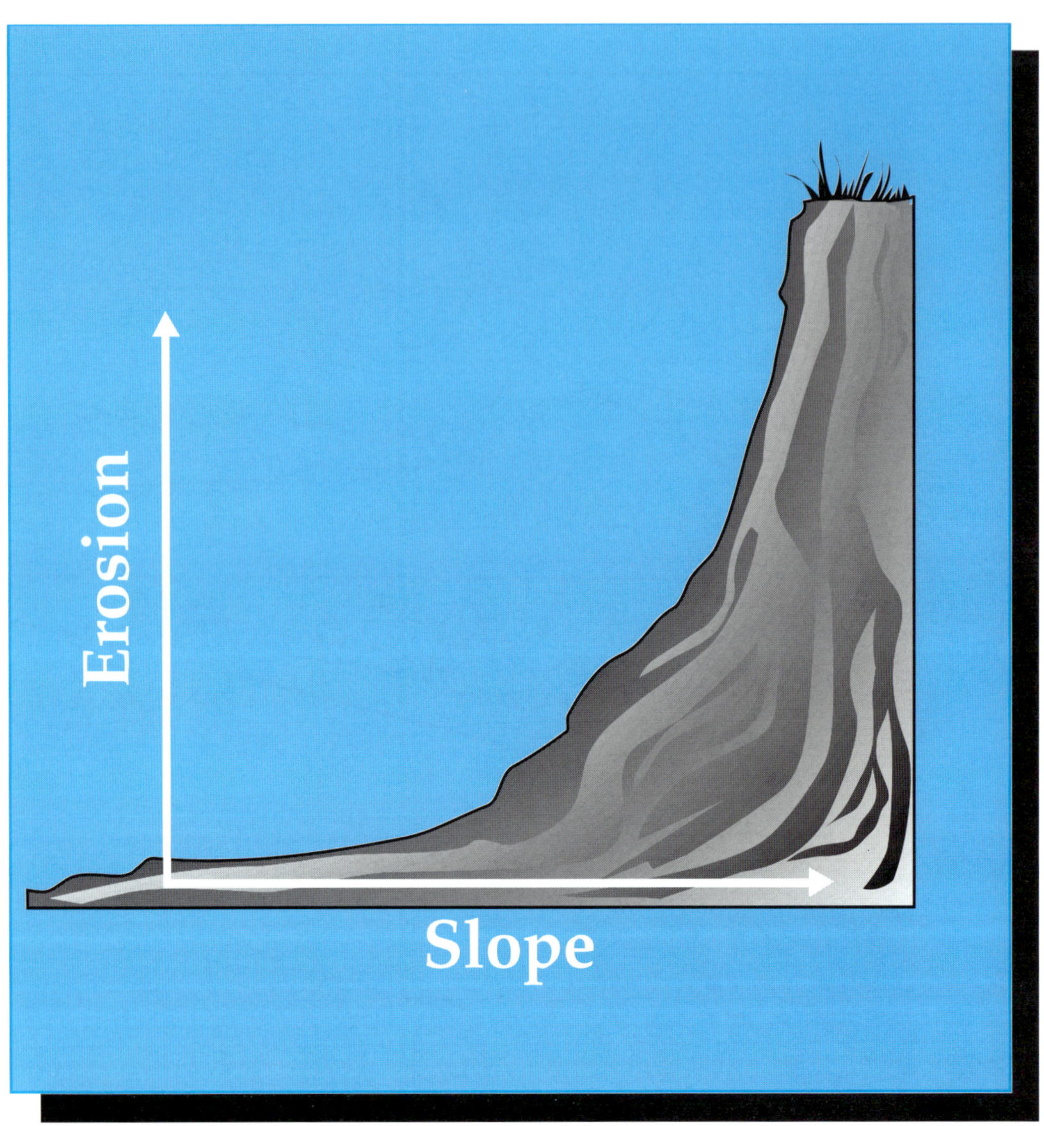

The steeper the slope, the greater the erosion

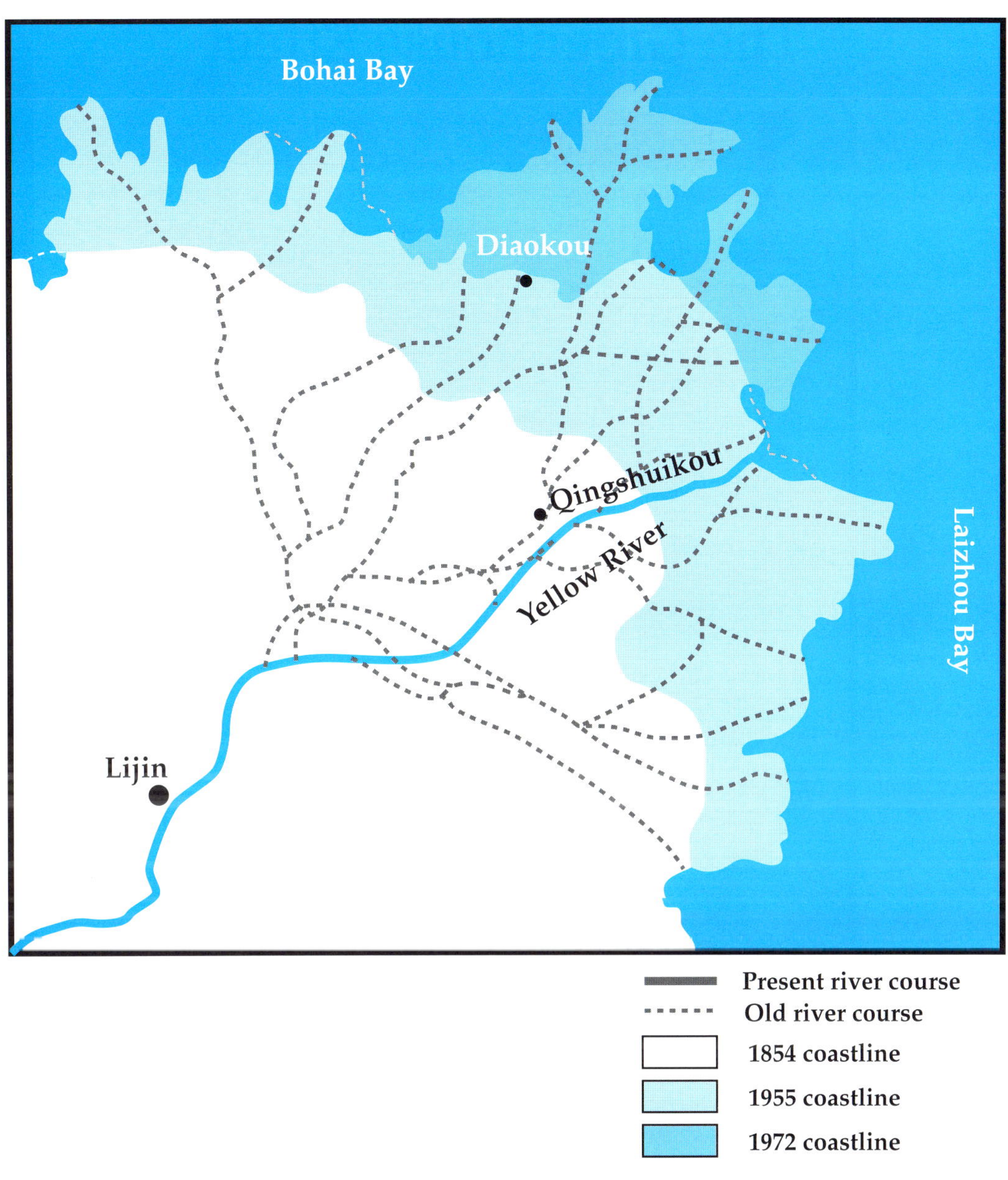

Siltation alters a coastline. Changes at the outlet of the Yellow River between 1855 and 1976

The Greenhouse Effect

In its history, the earth has gone through warm periods and through cold periods, called ice ages. There is strong evidence that it is now going through a warming period. Industrial burning of oil, gas, and coal has resulted in a buildup of the gas carbon dioxide (CO_2) in the atmosphere. CO_2 slows the escape of heat from the earth, causing the earth to grow warmer.

The average world temperature is likely to increase by between 1.5 and 4.5 degrees Celsius by the year 2030. Some scientists believe that the ice caps of Antarctica and the Arctic will melt and that this will result in flooding all around the Pacific.

With higher temperatures would come dramatic climatic changes. Some areas would have more rain, some less. Places with a subtropical climate would eventually become tropical, and deserts would start to bloom. Some places that are now fertile would become deserts because of lack of rain.

Carbon dioxide is a natural fertilizer. As a result, when there is a lot of carbon dioxide in the atmosphere, plants grow faster and become larger. Some scientists believe that carbon dioxide levels will double later in the next century. If they do, the yields of many crops and weeds will be as much as one-third greater than they are now.

A few thousand years ago people used to walk from the mainland to the Keppel Islands off the Australian coast. Then the sea level rose.

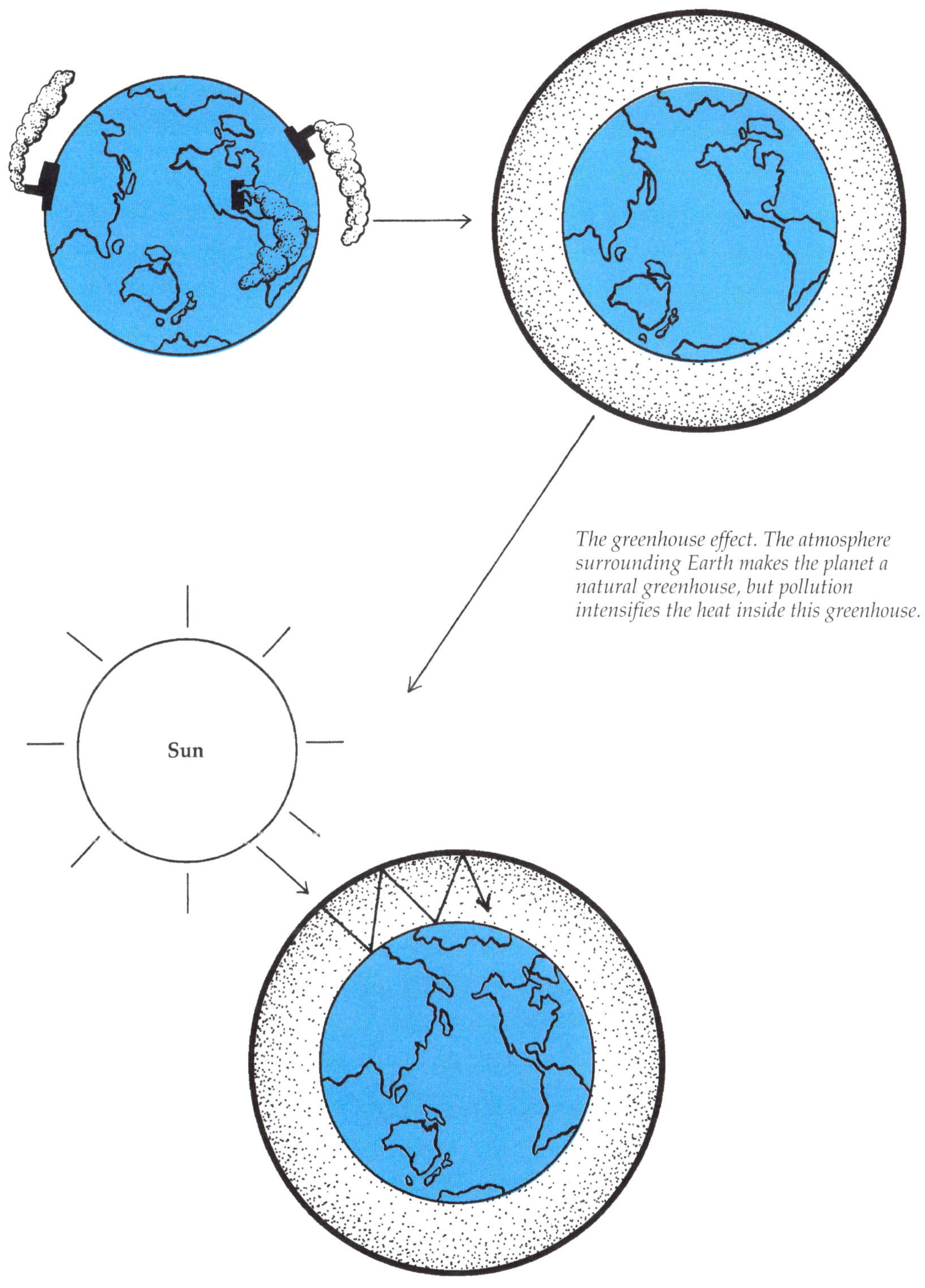

The greenhouse effect. The atmosphere surrounding Earth makes the planet a natural greenhouse, but pollution intensifies the heat inside this greenhouse.

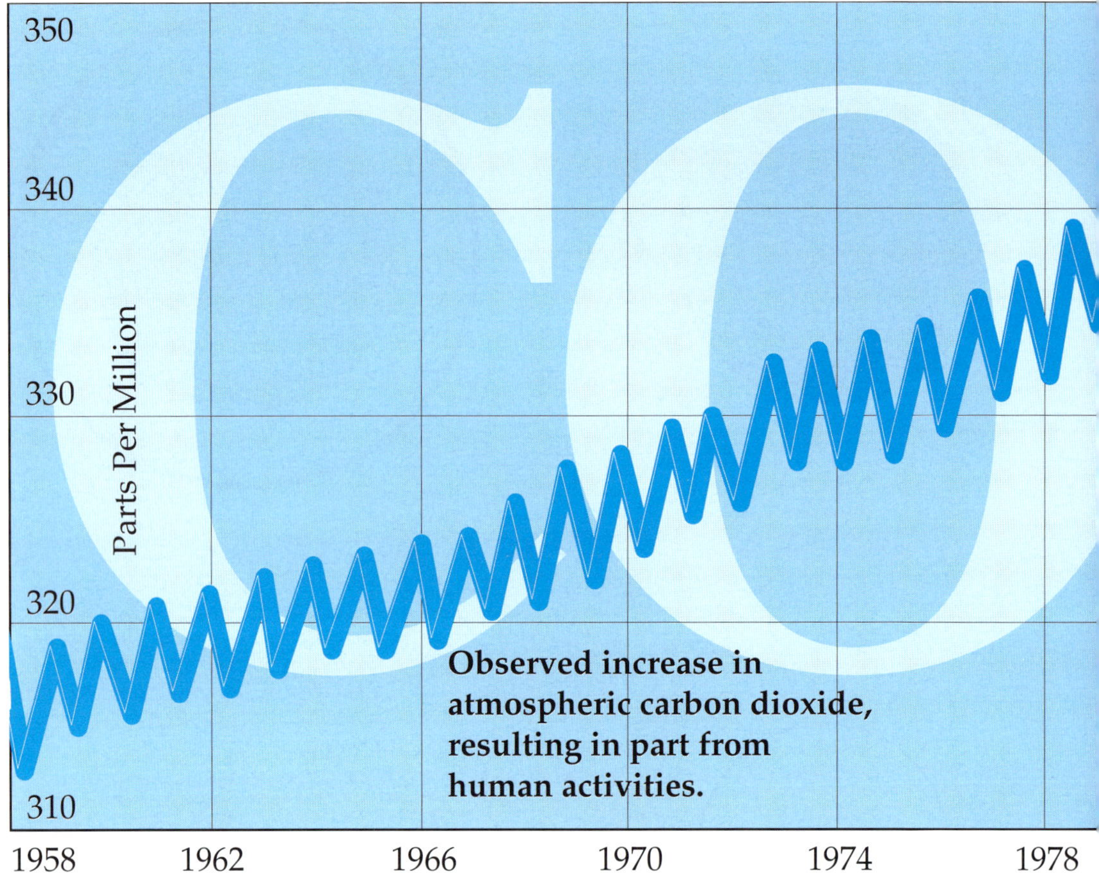

The climate of the world is so complicated that weather bureaus have a problem predicting the weather even from day to day. To predict a long-range change in climate is vastly more difficult. Since a rise or fall in sea level depends on the climate, it too is hard to predict. A rise in temperature would result in more evaporation; as a result, there would be changes in rainfall and in groundwater levels. Because of all this, scientists tend to be reluctant to predict the degree of flooding in particular places, although some are willing to take a guess at the average rise in sea level. Some scientists believe that by the year 2050, the sea level will be about one meter higher than it was in the 1980s. Others think that ocean levels will in fact lower as the water of the oceans evaporates and falls again as snow at the poles.

A rise in the level of the ocean would threaten much of the population of the world. Most of the cities in the world are near the coast. Atolls have grown up out of the sea, and their islands are mostly just above sea level. Even a 50-centimeter rise in the sea level would be disastrous. There would be a flood of refugees looking for new homes as their islands washed away.

1982
1986

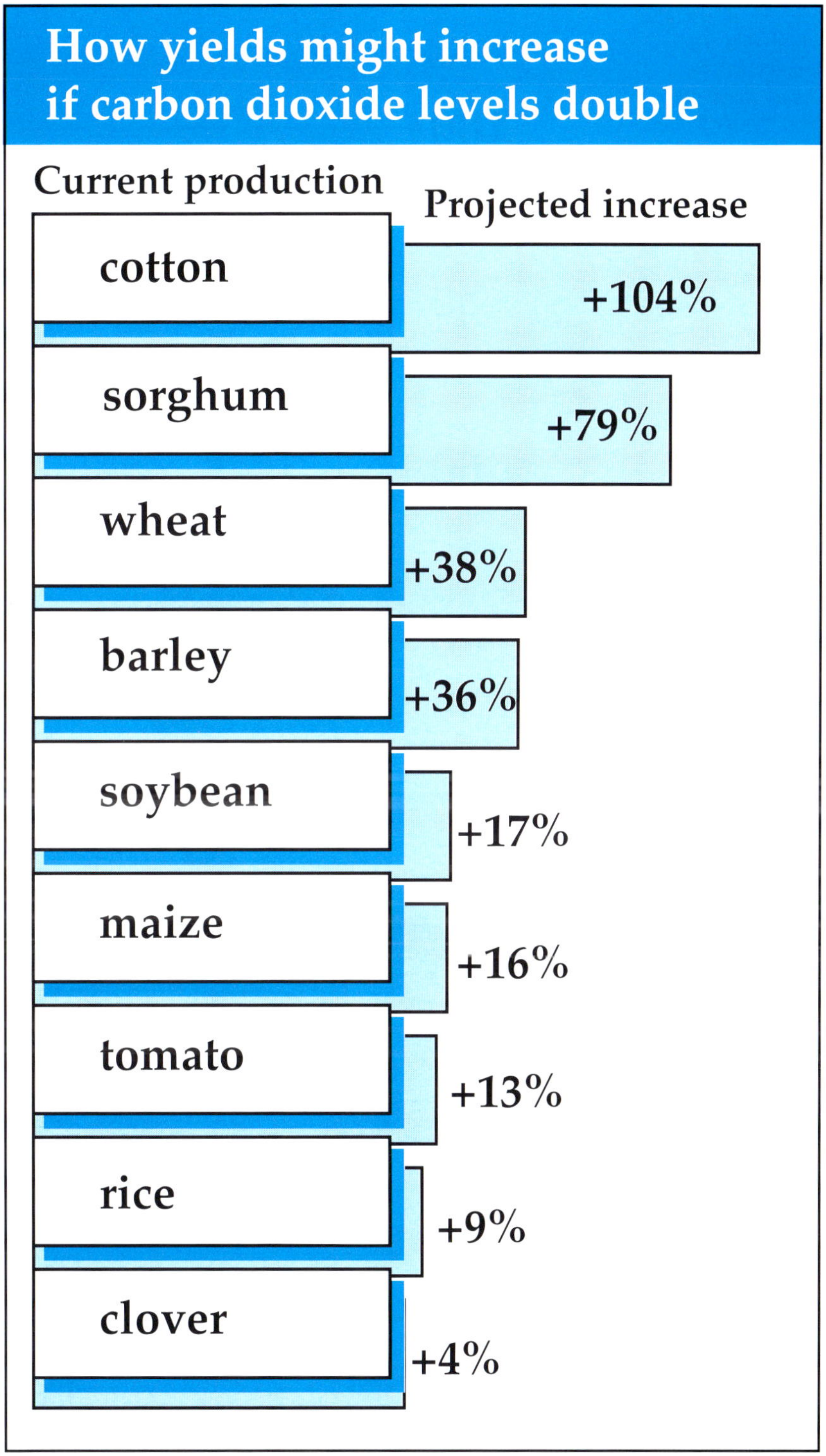
How yields might increase
if carbon dioxide levels double
Current production
Projected increase
cotton
+104%
sorghum
+79%
wheat
+38%
barley
+36%
soybean
+17%
maize
+16%
tomato
+13%
rice
+9%
clover
+4%

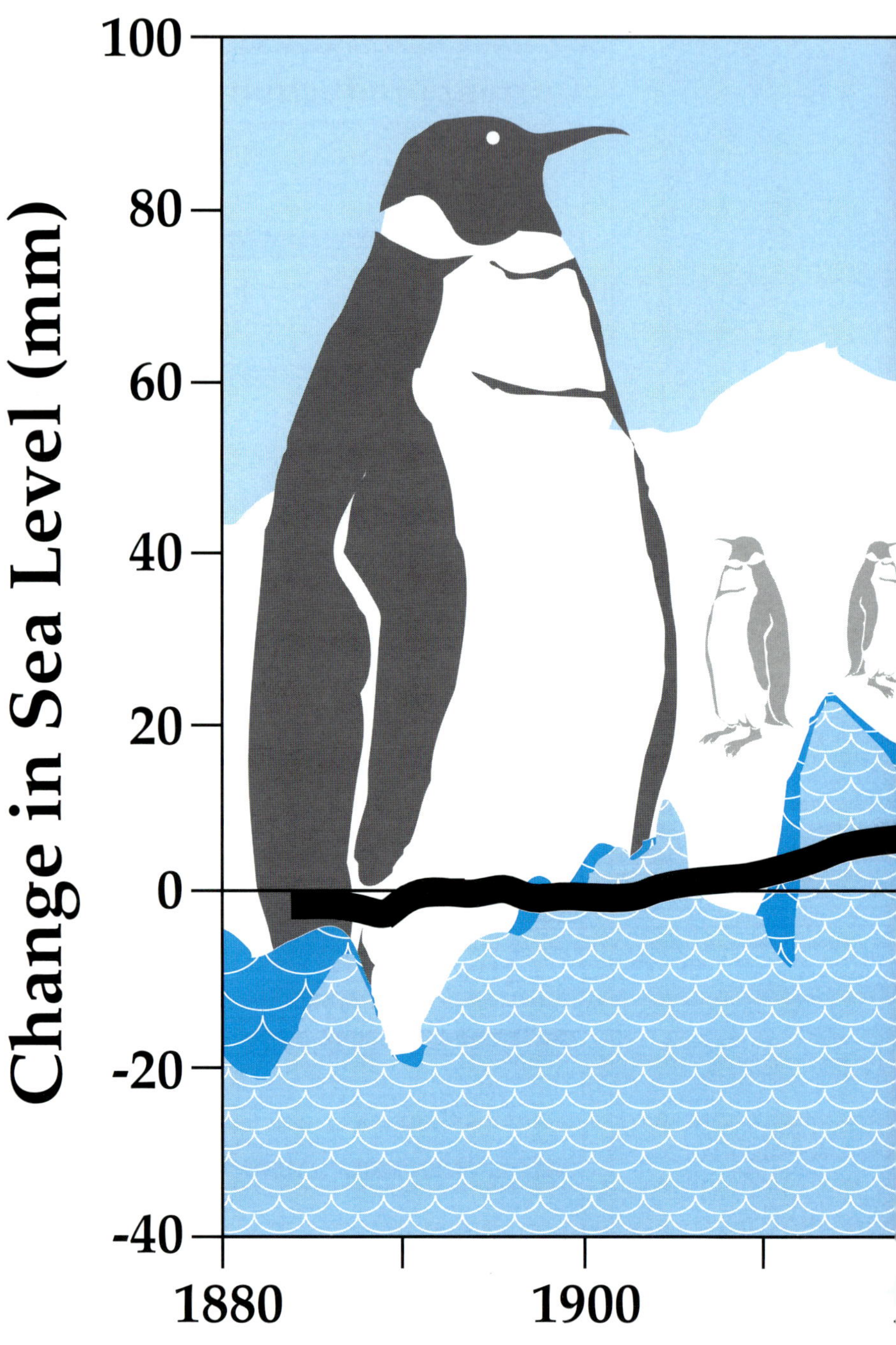

Changes in sea level since 1880. The heavy solid line shows global sea level change caused by the melting of small glaciers. The dark sea above it shows the estimated changes in sea level caused by the increased volume of carbon dioxide in the air, which in turn raises the temperature of the ocean. As water heats, it expands and actually stands taller. The light-colored sea shows where sea level would be without the effects of this thermal expansion.

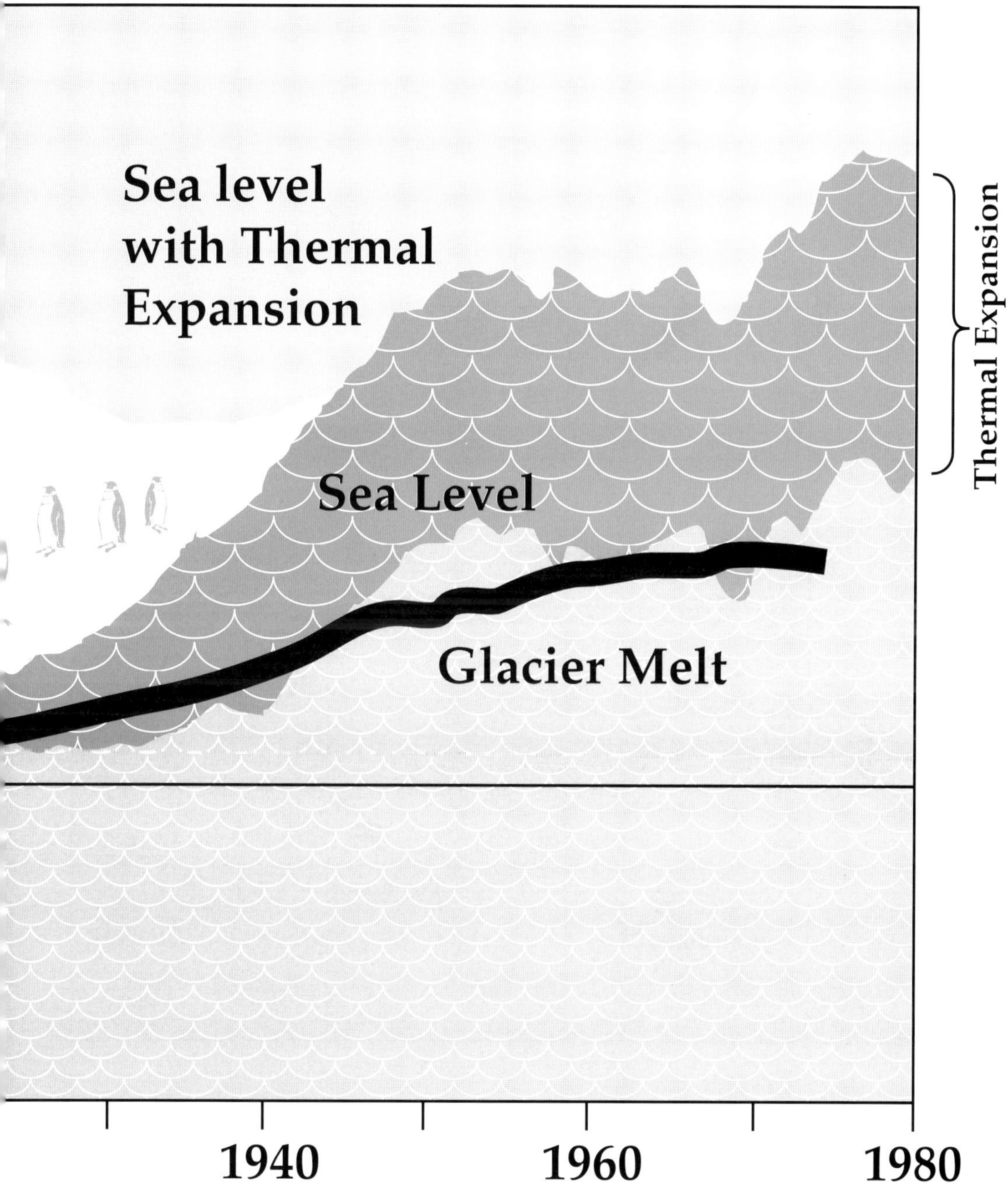

Sea level
with Thermal
Expansion
Sea Level
Glacier Melt
Thermal Expansion
1940
1960
1980

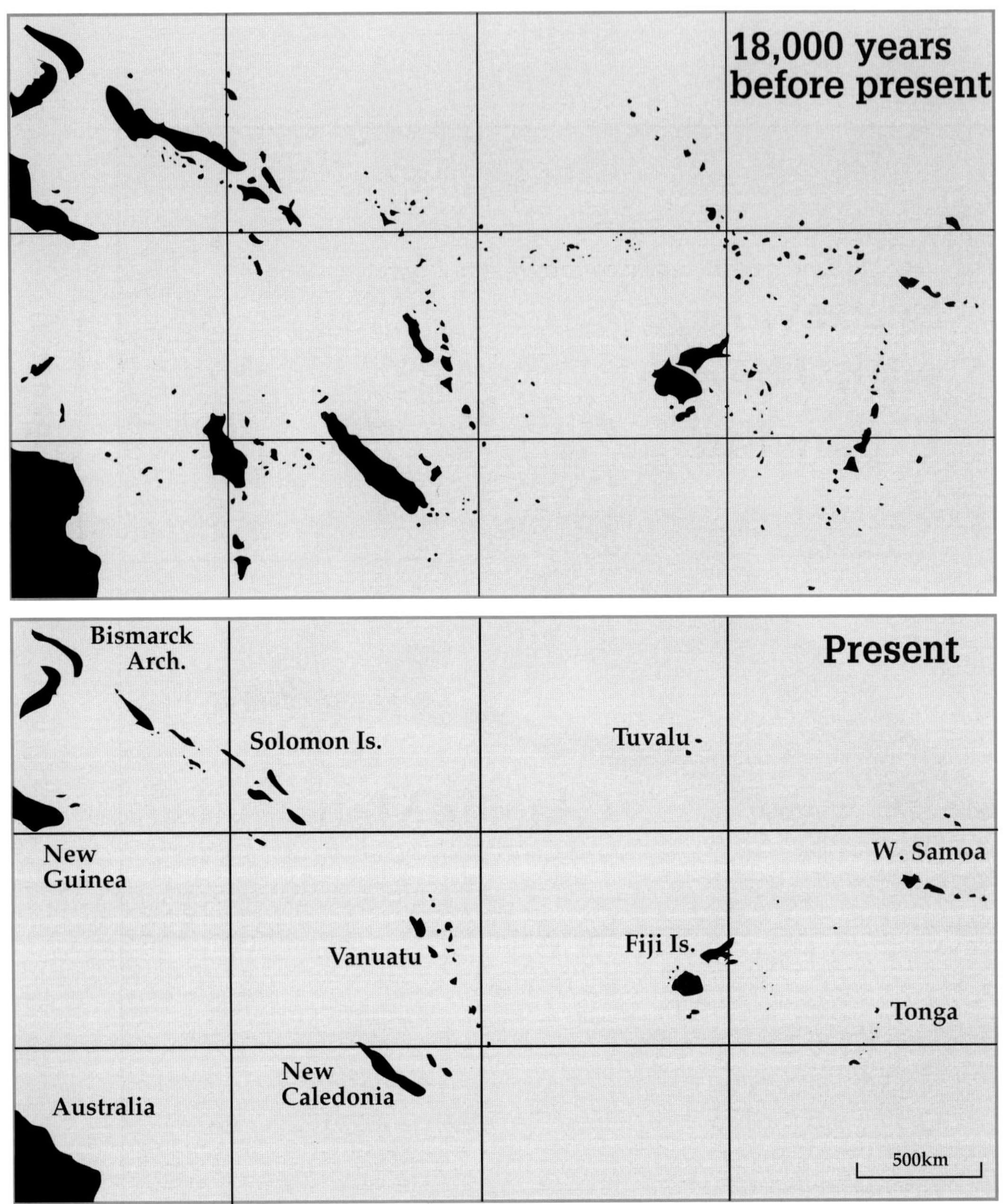

*Southwest Pacific coastline at glacial maximum 18,000 years ago
(upper drawing) and during the past 4,000 years (lower drawing)*

The Ozone Layer

What Is the Ozone Layer?

When we get sunburned, it is not from the heat or the light of the sun, but from its ultraviolet rays. We wear polarized sunglasses to filter out the ultraviolet radiation that damages our eyes. People who live in sunny countries wrinkle earlier than those who live where the sun does not shine much. Their skins age faster. This is particularly true of people with fair skin. In northern Australia, over 80 percent of the population get skin cancer at some time in their lives because they have skins that cannot cope with the sun. They are living where they do not belong. All these problems are going to get worse.

High in the atmosphere is a gas called ozone (O_3). It surrounds the earth like a delicate veil, protecting it and us from the ultraviolet rays of the sun. The veil is very thin indeed. If all the ozone were collected at the surface of the earth, it would form a layer only about 3 millimeters thick. Because there is so little of it, it is very easy to destroy.

The ozone layer—less ozone means more ultraviolet light.

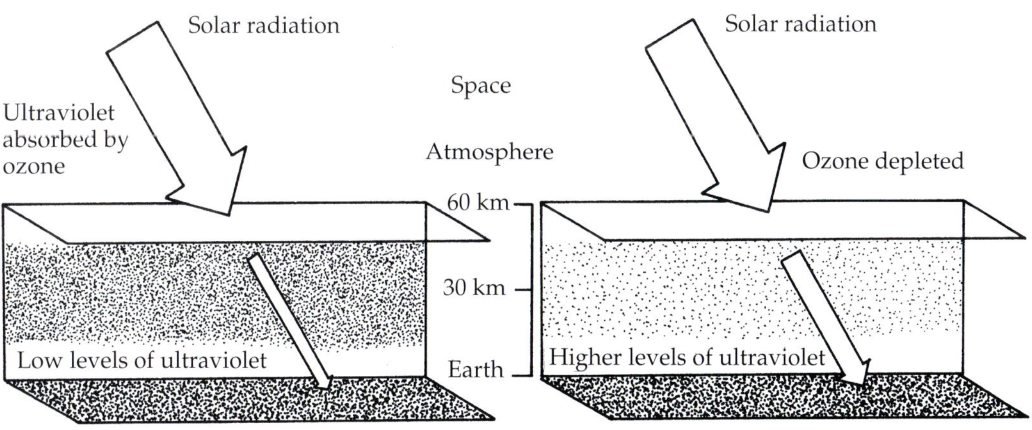

What Has Happened to the Ozone Layer?

A number of chemicals used in industry and in our homes break down ozone and potentially reduce or deplete the ozone layer. The most important are called chlorofluorocarbons (CFC). Unfortunately CFCs are very useful chemicals. They are used in refrigeration, without which large quantities of food would be wasted. The foam rubber or foam plastic used to make a great variety of things (sponges, mattresses, insulating boxes in which you buy fast food, foam cups that keep tea and coffee warm) is made with CFC. CFC was once widely used in aerosol sprays, but a number of countries have banned or greatly reduced its use. Japan uses one-third of the CFCs produced in the world.

In the spring of 1989, there was 40 percent less ozone above the Antarctic than in 1957. Most of this change has happened since the mid-1970s. In the spring, there is a hole in the ozone over the Antarctic. Ozone depletion is likely to occur elsewhere in the world, as well.

Chlorofluorocarbons in the atmosphere

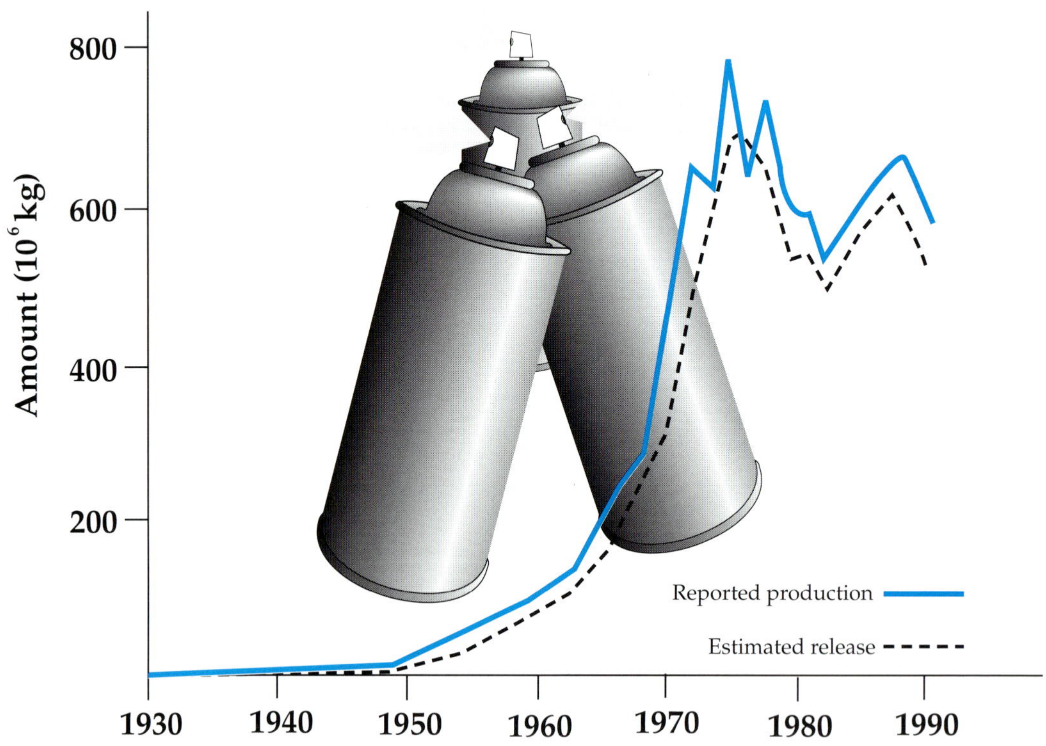

What Are the Effects of Less Ozone?

Changes of a few percent in such a delicate veil would be enough to let through much more ultraviolet. For example, a 10 percent reduction in the layer would let through 20 percent more ultraviolet. It is thought that by the year 2050, the ozone layer will have been depleted by a few more percent.

As well as directly affecting humans by causing sunburn, snow blindness, eye damage, skin cancer, and the ageing and wrinkling of skin, ultraviolet rays do other harm. They slow down plant growth. Trees and grasses are particularly badly affected, but crops are too. While the greenhouse effect is expected to cause an increase in plant growth, ozone depletion is expected to reduce it. Ultraviolet rays kill algae and the fish that feed on them. More ultraviolet would mean fewer fish to catch. Ultraviolet rays also cause paints to fade, window glass to turn yellow, and car roofs to go chalky. The depletion of the ozone layer would cause more smog, and with higher temperatures brought about by the greenhouse effect, the resulting atmosphere would be even more uncomfortable. Acid rain would also increase.

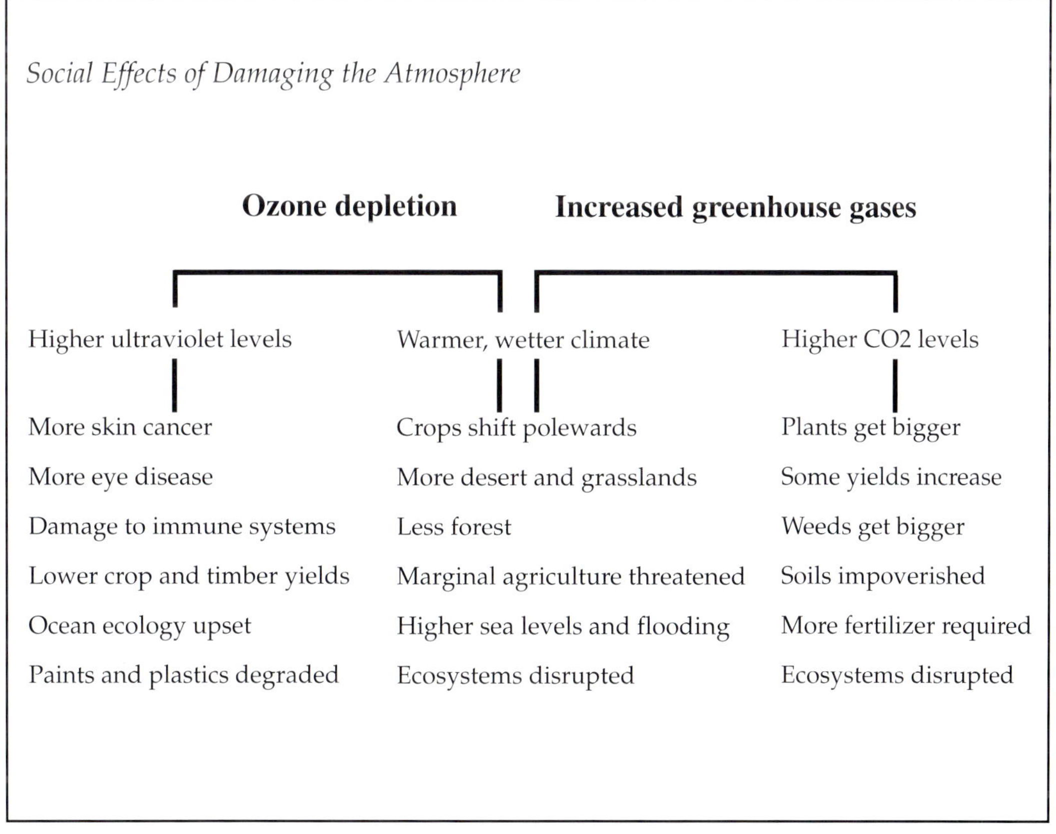

So What Can We Do?

The atmosphere of the earth is being damaged by CFCs, and unnecessary use should be stopped. You can help by checking labels on spray cans to see that chlorine compounds are not used in them and by refusing to buy any products containing chloro-fluorocarbons.

Because ultraviolet radiation damages living things, you should avoid being exposed to high levels of it. Take precautions in summer: wear a sun hat and use sun block, especially if you have fair skin.

Scientists have identified the ozone hole, the greenhouse effect, and acid rain, and we have now become more aware of the extent of the large-scale damage that people have done to the earth. For the first time, nations of the world see the need to reduce the dangers that threaten all of us. Already many governments have signed an international agreement to protect the ozone layer.

Coastal Management

Who Owns the Beach?

More than two-thirds of the population of the world lives within 80 kilometers of the coast, and yet in many countries, access to the beach is not a right.

Australia

The Australian public has access to most of the Australian coast, since in most places the coastal strip (often only 100 meters wide) belongs to the government. This is because most of the land in Australia was not bought and sold until the nineteenth century, after people had begun to think about the importance of water and access to the coast. Before land was sold, therefore, local governments had plans that showed all the waterways and beaches as "Crown land." In most cases they have stayed that way. The public does not have access to Aboriginal reserves because they are for tribal Aboriginal people who live by hunting and gathering their food.

Australia is extremely rich in minerals. During the 1960s and 1970s, when it was found that the Great Barrier Reef was a really good place to find oil, the Queensland government granted

The Gold Coast, Australia, a major tourist resort. The canals that are now used for marinas are where the mangroves used to be.

drilling licences to various oil companies. The state government granted the licences; however, the federal government withdrew them, put the Great Barrier Reef onto the World Heritage list, and made it into a marine park.

Costa Rica

In 1977, the government of Costa Rica passed a law declaring that the first 200 meters inland from mean sea level is part of the national heritage. Some land was excluded from the law (for example, national parks and land purchased privately before 1977), but 75 percent of the shore remains a public zone.

Japan

In Japan, most of the coastline is developed. Tokyo Bay, where almost none of the natural coastline is left, is the most extreme example. The coastline has been "reclaimed." That is, people have dumped huge amounts of rubbish or other material on the shore and built it up until it has become land.

The result is that people in Japan who want to go fishing for fun, generally do not go to the sea. If they are lucky there may be a lake or pond nearby.

There may also be nearby a dam owned by somebody whose business it is to keep it stocked with fish. There people sit, catching fish in the center of the city.

Mexico

Mexico has a federal coastal zone. On beaches, this zone includes the intertidal zone and 20 meters inland. In the case of cliffs or rocky shores, the zone embraces the cliffs or shores themselves and the 20 meters inland from the first point on which people can freely walk.

The federal coastal zone is considered public property and thus cannot be bought or owned by anyone. However, just beyond this zone, most of the land is private property, and so the area of beach or shore that the public can use is actually quite small.

New Zealand

In New Zealand the foreshore is open public space and people must be free to land there. A small percentage of it is privately owned. Where this is the case, it must be returned to the state when the land is sold.

The "Queen's Chain" extends 22 yards (about 20 meters) above the high-water line. It applies to the whole coastline of New Zealand and belongs to the people of New Zealand.

USA

Most states own the beach between high and low water (the "wet sand"), but getting to the beach is not always an easy matter. On the mainland United States, 72 percent of the Pacific coast above the high-water line is privately owned. In Oregon, a "permanent public easement" allows the public to use most of the dry sand beach, even that which is privately owned. In California, on the other hand, there is much less public access.

With the passage of the national Coastal Zone Management Act, the trend throughout the United States has been toward increasing public access to beaches.

The Sacred Sea

To the Maori people of New Zealand, the sea is sacred, or *tapu*. This is because it is vital to the people's lives as a source of food. Historically, the Maoris had laws that helped conserve the environment of the sea and thus keep it and them clean. These laws varied from place to place. The people did not dare to anger the Guardian of the Sea, Tangaroa, and they would offer a prayer before going down to the sea.

Some of the laws were as follows:

- When going down to the sea, you had to have a clean body, clean hair, and clean thoughts.
- No body wastes could enter the sea from the beach.
- You were allowed to fish only at certain times. The Maori calendar is still an excellent guide to the best times to go fishing.
- Seafood always had to be a certain size.
- You had to return to their original place any stones or rocks you had upturned.
- You could not plunder the sea. You took only as much as you needed.
- You had to return your first fish to Tangaroa as an offering. You were not allowed to turn you back on Tangaroa.
- In some places you could not eat seafood on the beach. You had to take it home and prepare and eat it there.

All of the laws of *tapu* reinforce the belief that the sea is an invaluable resource that must be treated with care and respect.

Fishing Regulations

Animals from the sea are part of the diet of most Pacific people. Koreans get about 80 percent of their protein from marine animals, Pacific islanders about 60 percent, and Japanese about 40 percent, while Australians, New Zealanders and Americans get 4 percent to 10 percent.

There are over two billion people for whom the Pacific Ocean is a source of protein. The larger nations of the Pacific have fishing fleets that travel far and wide to satisfy the needs of home markets. But since 90 percent of all fish are found in coastal zones, these fleets must operate in the waters of other nations, and other nations often do not like to give "their" fish away.

A nation that does not want its waters fished by other nations has a difficult task in policing them. The areas of open sea to be patrolled are enormous. Even a nation like the United States that can use satellites and aircraft for surveillance has great difficulty in finding and catching poachers.

Where nations of the Pacific do allow other nations to fish in their waters, they usually

*Pacific fish catch in metric tons, 1992. (*Pacific Islands included: Solomons, Fiji, New Caledonia, Micronesia, Samoa, Vanuatu, French Polynesia, Tonga, Palau, Cook Islands, Guam, Northern Marianas, Marshall Islands, and Niue.)*

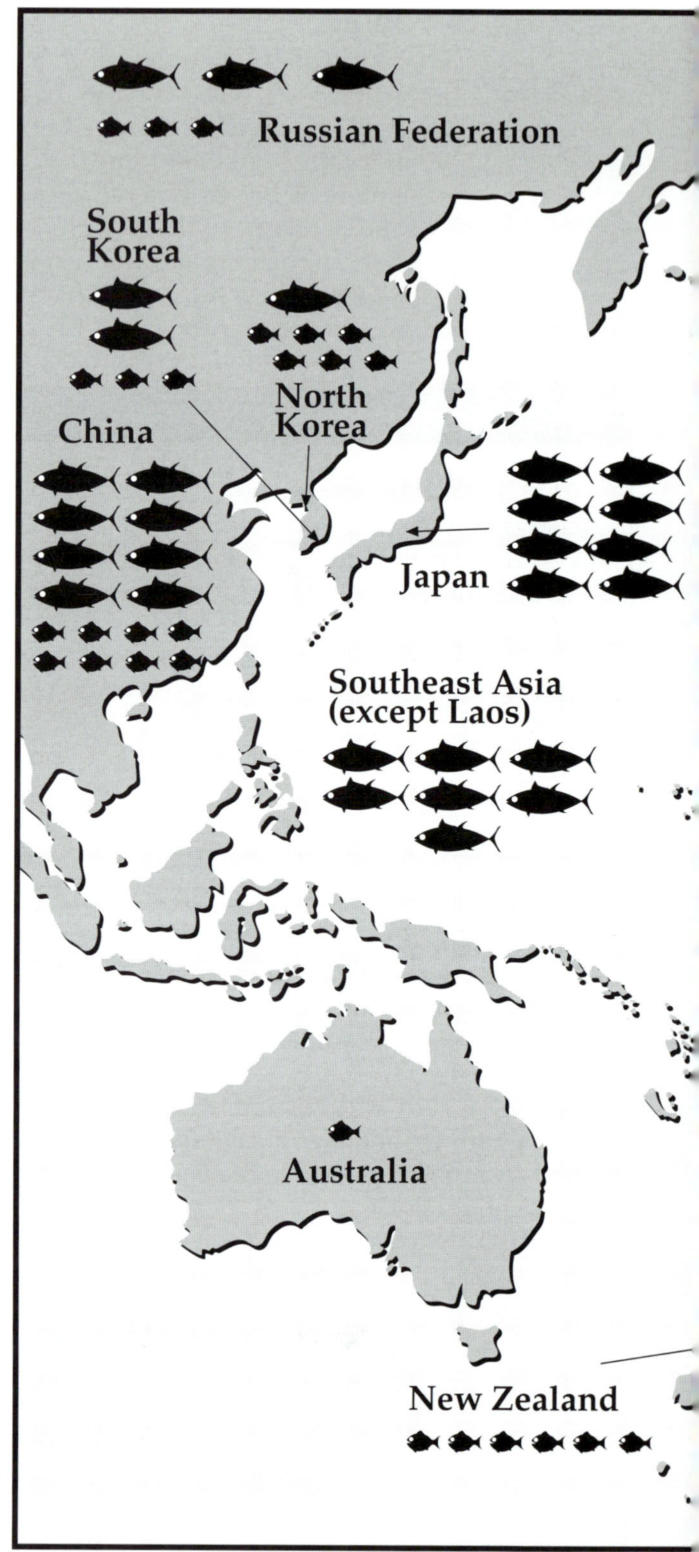

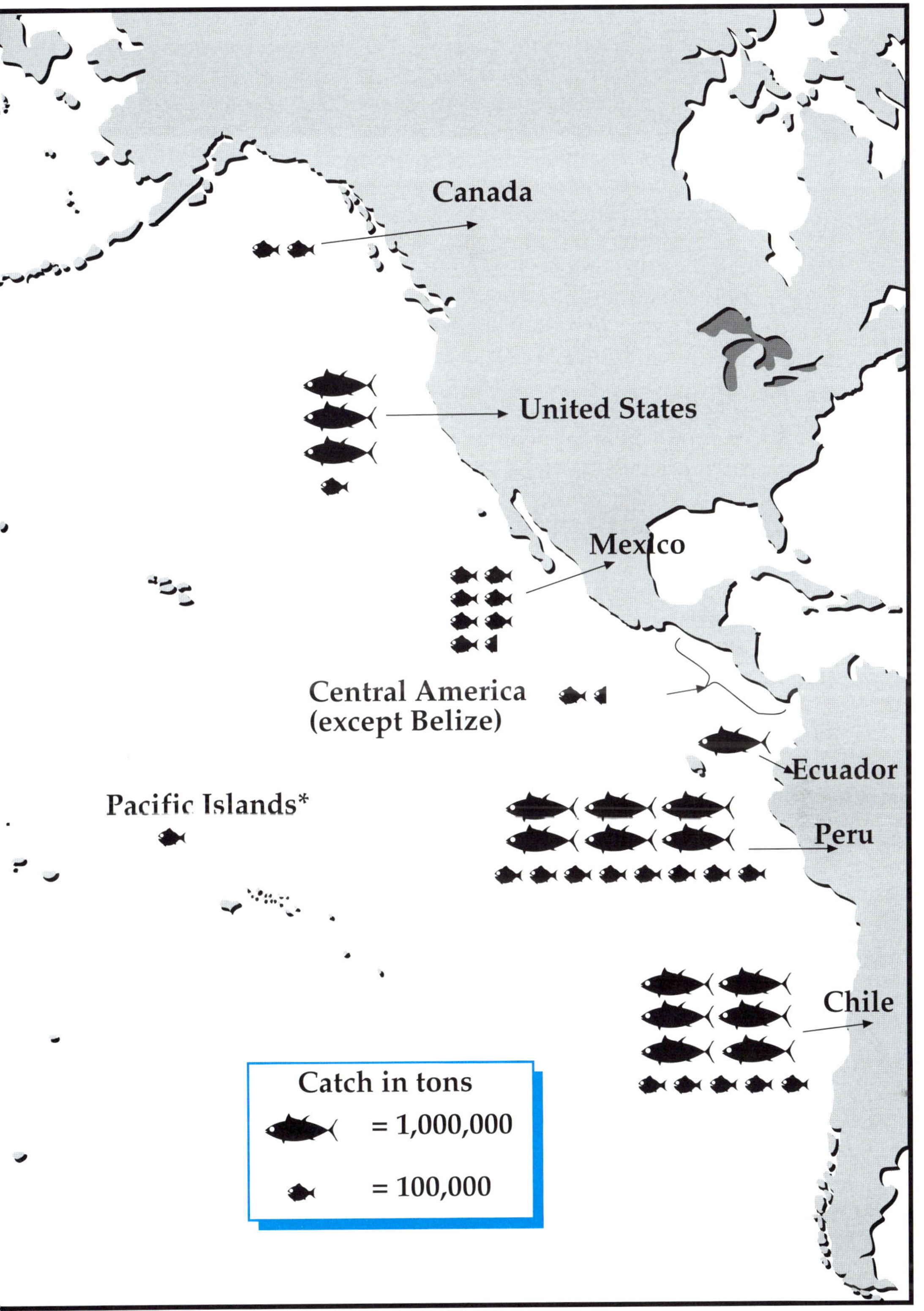

Canada
United States
Mexico
Central America
(except Belize)
Ecuador
Peru
Pacific Islands*
Chile
Catch in tons
= 1,000,000
= 100,000

control the catch carefully. Sometimes they make treaties in which all parties agree on the controls. The United States and Canada jointly regulate salmon fishing along parts of their Pacific coasts. Many Pacific island nations have fishing agreements with Japan, Korea, the United States, and other countries. Sometimes nations control fishing by licensing foreign companies and individual fishing boats. Sometimes fees are paid to local governments by factory ships that receive the catches of local fishers.

As well as controlling fishing by other nations, most countries regulate the kind and amount of fish that their own people may harvest. If they allow overfishing, the economic usefulness of a population can be quickly destroyed. For some 50 years, sardines off the California coast provided jobs for thousands of people who caught and processed them. Today the great schools of these tiny fish are no longer found and the industry is gone. This kind of depletion is happening more and more throughout the Pacific. Governments try to prevent this destruction in a number of ways:

- *Limiting numbers:* Governments grant or sell licenses that limit the number of people, vessels, and companies that may engage in harvesting. Often these permits have other restrictions controlling the amount and kind of animals that may be taken and the way they may be caught.

- *Limiting the time:* Governments decide when fishing is allowed and when it is not. By declaring a season in this way, they can protect animal populations when they most need protection, particularly during spawning. It is also a way of limiting the amount of the catch.

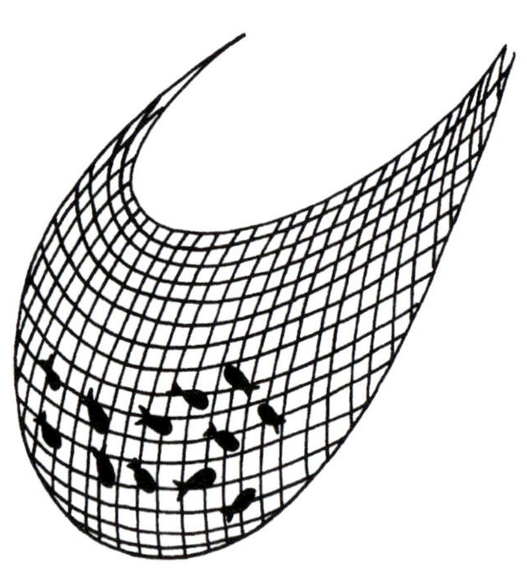

- *Limiting the catch:* Governments restrict the total weight of the catch. In the case of turtles and furbearing mammals (such as fur seals), the limit may be on the number that may be taken.

- *Limiting the gear:* Every kind of harvesting gear can be controlled.

Net size: Governments dictate the length, total area, and mesh size of nets. Mesh size determines the size of fish caught. The larger the mesh the larger the fish because small fish can swim through large openings.

Number of hooks: When regulations restrict the number of hooks on a line, the number of fish that can be taken at any one time is limited, and this means that more escape.

Size of vessel: Large vessels can carry more fuel and food and they can store a larger catch, so they can stay at sea longer than smaller ones. Therefore, limiting the size of the vessel limits the size of the catch.

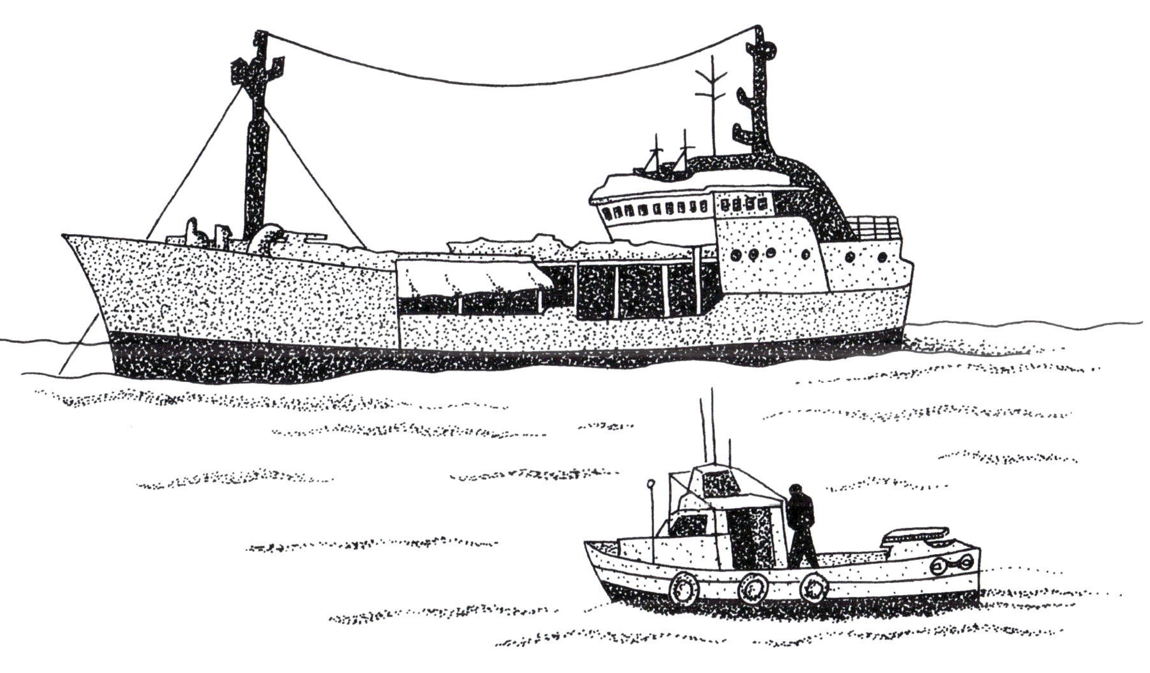

For centuries many peoples of the world have raised fish in ponds. Ponds are normally owned by individuals and companies, and governments do not control the harvest. However, in recent times, marine "farmers" have been releasing turtles, eels, and salmon that go into the open ocean to graze or breed and then return to their hatcheries, where they are harvested. This kind of ocean "ranching" is only now gaining legal protection.

All along the coast of China, clams, mussels, oysters, shrimp, prawns, and edible seaweed are raised. This aquaculture began during the Song dynasty (960 to 1126 AD), at about the time the Normans conquered England.

Between 1960 and 1986, the amount of pond-raised fish produced in China increased by eight even though the area of ponds increased by only three.

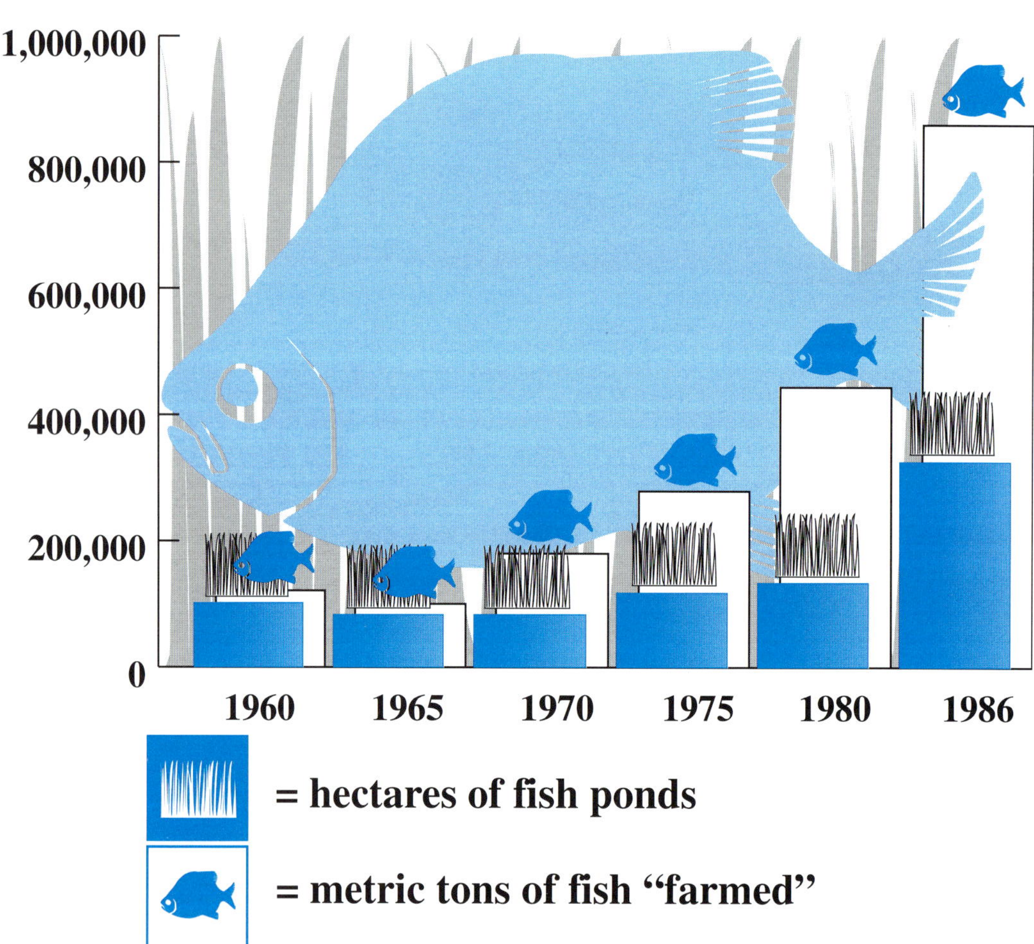

Original Peoples

Who Are Original Peoples?

Forty thousand years ago, when Australia was joined to Asia, the forebears of the Australian Aborigines came through Indonesia to Australia. Then the land they had crossed sank beneath the sea. In the next 39,700 years, they saw some traders from Malaysia who came to gather sea cucumbers to sell as medicine in China; some fishers from Papua New Guinea; and perhaps a few Chinese and European explorers. It is not surprising that although they thought of themselves as members of a particular tribe, they had no name for themselves as a nation. They called themselves "people." This is why they were given the name "aboriginal." In Latin, "ab" means "from." They are "from the original people."

The Polynesians made epic voyages in their great canoes to settle the uninhabited volcanic islands and coral atolls of the Pacific. Thousands of years ago they came from the islands round Tahiti to Hawaii. Before that they had traveled from the Indonesian area to Tonga, Samoa, New Zealand and other Pacific islands. Their languages are all obviously the same Polynesian language. "Poly" means "many," and "nesos," "island." They are the people of the many islands.

Three hundred years ago, the Japanese began to move north, fighting the original people of the Japanese Archipelago, the Ainu, and conquering the northern half of the island of Honshu. It is thought that the place name Mount Fuji, which represents Japan to the world, comes from the Ainu word meaning a volcano. The word Ainu comes from a word meaning "people of the sword."

Three hundred years ago, Chinese people from Fujian began migrating to the island of Formosa, which is now called Taiwan, displacing the Formosan people whose language is related to the Polynesian languages.

The ancestors of the Indians of North and South America moved across the Bering Strait from Asia between 30 and 50 thousand years ago. They formed many different peoples.

In the 1500s, the Spaniards colonized South America and in the 1600s British settlements grew up on the Atlantic coast of North America. For a couple of hundred years, European explorers had been merely passing through the Pacific. A few European traders lived in China and Japan, and in Indonesia, where they traded in spices, but it was not until about two hundred years ago that the Europeans came to the Pacific to stay.

Original peoples of the Pacific and their present ways of life. The figures in parentheses represent percentage of total population.

Ainu
50,000 (0.02%)
Southeast Asian
tribal peoples
18 million
Philippine tribal people
6.5 million (16%)
Aborigines
250,000 (2%)

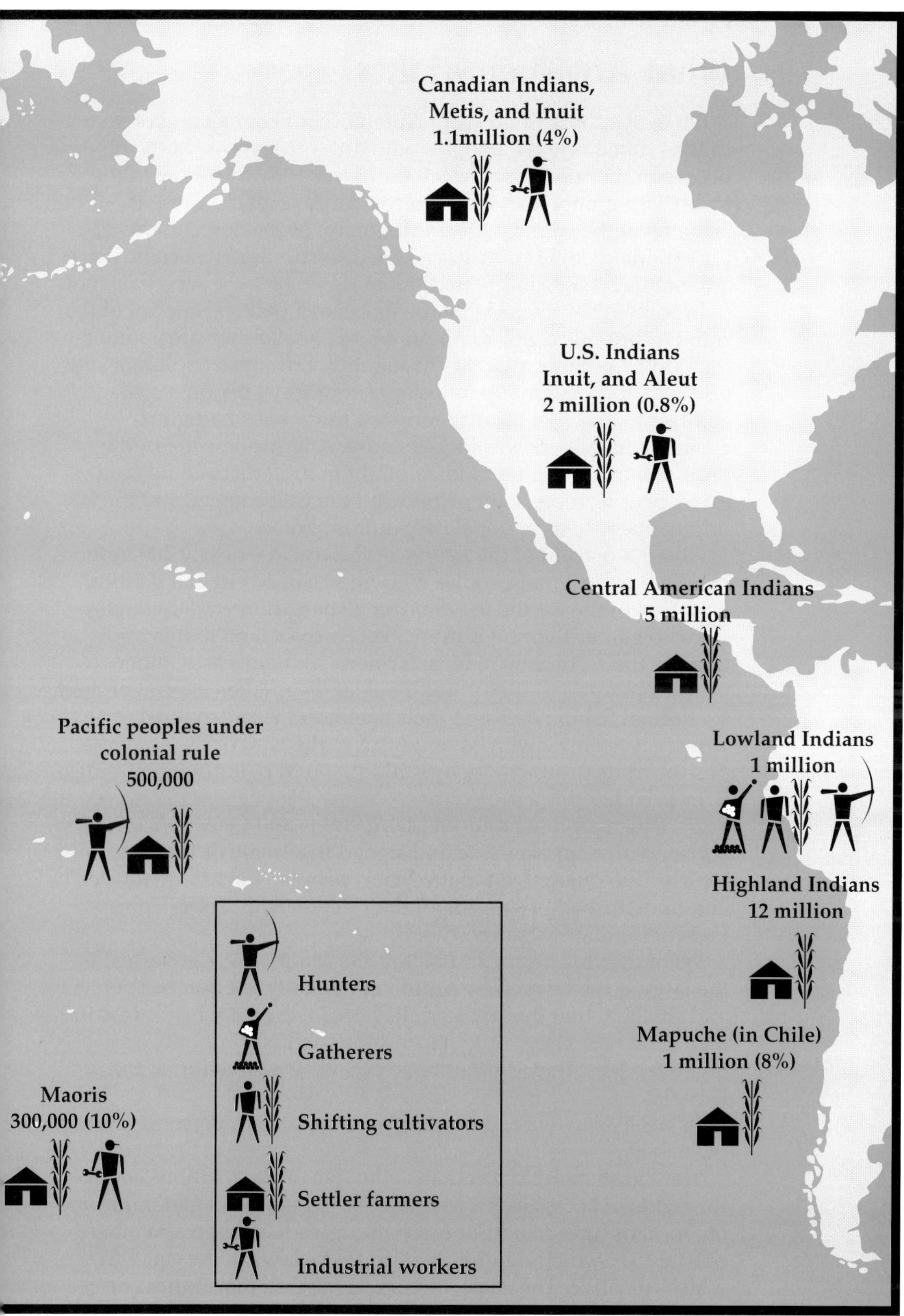

Canadian Indians,
Metis, and Inuit
1.1million (4%)

U.S. Indians
Inuit, and Aleut
2 million (0.8%)

Central American Indians
5 million

Pacific peoples under
colonial rule
500,000

Lowland Indians
1 million

Highland Indians
12 million

Mapuche (in Chile)
1 million (8%)

Maoris
300,000 (10%)

Hunters
Gatherers
Shifting cultivators
Settler farmers
Industrial workers

What Are Their Rights?

On every continent (except Antarctica, of course) and on many islands dwell original peoples who differ from most of the other people in the country in which they live. They live more in the style of their ancestors than in accordance with the present fashions of the country. Of course, many of the descendants of the original peoples may have joined the dominant society. We are interested here in the traditional rights of those who have not.

In some cases, the original peoples have political control of the country, but this is not common. More usually they are a minority. Why? Epidemic diseases brought by European explorers and settlers wiped out many thousands of original people in the eighteenth and nineteenth centuries. Europeans had guns, against which there was little defense. And in some areas, the productive farming methods brought in by settlers could feed many people; more settlers followed the first comers, and the original people were hopelessly outnumbered.

About 4 percent of the people of the world—nearly 200 million people—are original peoples who find themselves in a political minority. In the Pacific they may be fishers, hunters, or wanderers who gather their food from a vast area of land that is traditionally theirs, or they may be farmers. In many cases, other people have seized their traditional lands or taken control of their traditional fishing areas, so their livelihood is endangered. In worse cases, those who have control of the land or the sea have destroyed its productivity by building on it, polluting it, mining it, or even bombing it.

In 1840, over five hundred Maori chiefs and Queen Victoria's representative in New Zealand signed the Treaty of Waitangi. Article Two guaranteed to the Maori people "the full exclusive and undisturbed possession of their Lands and Estates Forests Fisheries and other properties."

What did this mean? In practice the Maoris were governed by the laws of the land. They could harvest only the number of fish and shellfish that the law said they could, except when it was for their own use. They could harvest the shellfish, but only according to the law. They did not have exclusive possession of the fisheries.

In 1989, a law was passed to give the Maoris a percentage of the fishery.

The North American Indians who live on reservations control the rights of access to the resources of the land and water they are on. Indians have in addition certain rights to salmon and other coastal fish, which exempt them from the laws of the states in which they live. The Alaskan Indians have similar rights.The

Inuit people of North America are allowed to hunt polar bears, even though the bears are otherwise protected. In Hawaii the Polynesian people have no special rights of access to coastal resources. In Australia tribal aboriginal people who live on the coast are allowed to take dugong for their own use, even though the dugong are otherwise totally protected by law.

When the Pacific became a nuclear testing ground, original peoples were particularly hard hit.

MICRONESIA
Micronesia has been a U.N. "strategic" Trust Territory administered by the U.S. since 1947.

• U.S. military plans to take over 1/3 of the land in opposition to popular Nuclear Free Constitution.

• U.S. colony and military base
• Base for Trident

• U.S. has taken 2/3 of island of Tinian as military base.

Guam
Belau
Rongelap

New
Caledonia

• Uranium mining on Aboriginal lands, destroying sacred sites, e.g., British Petroleum, Roxby Downs - Kokatha Land.
• British Nuclear Tests, 1940-1950s, left land contaminated and people suffering without compensation.

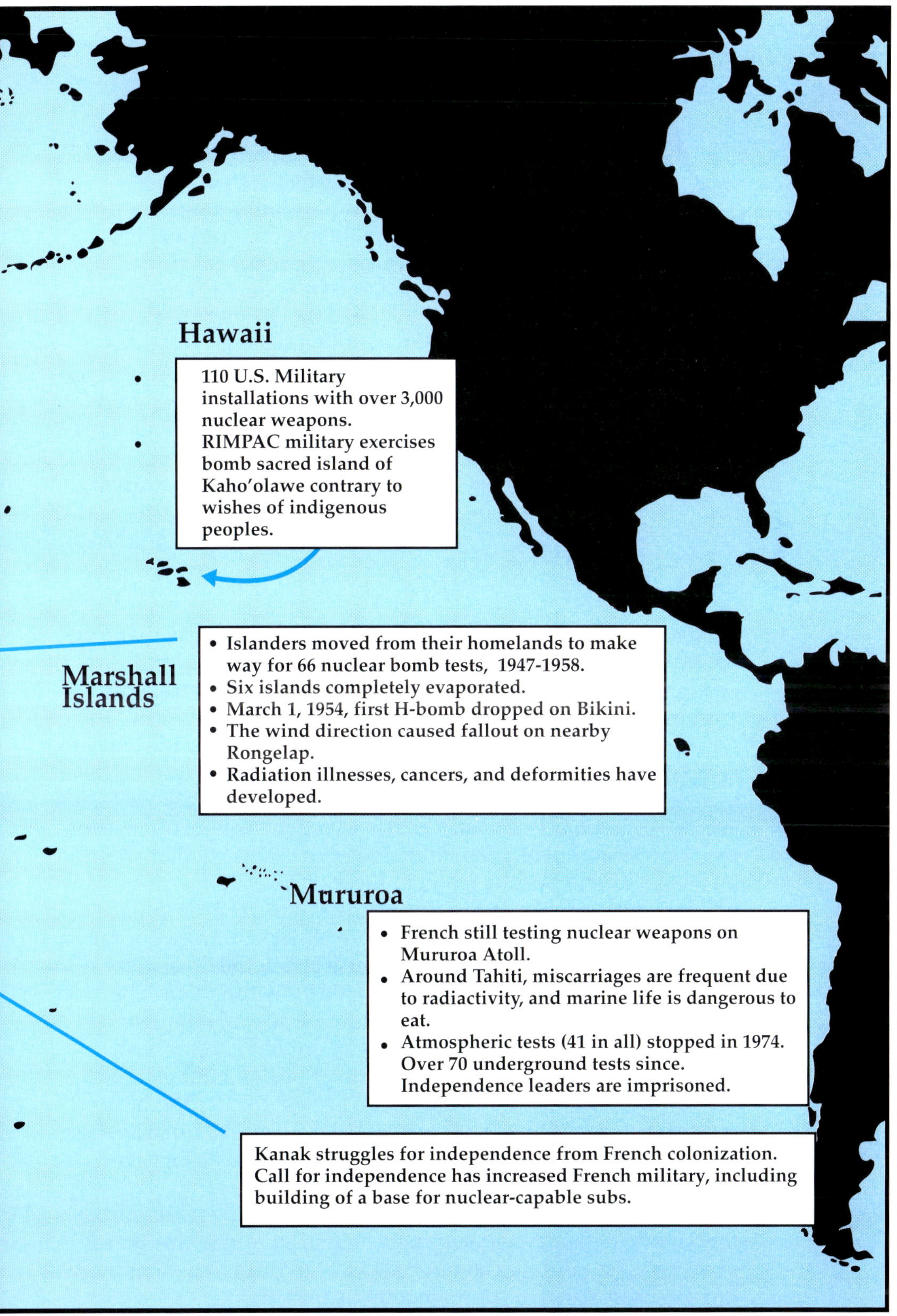

Hawaii

110 U.S. Military installations with over 3,000 nuclear weapons.
RIMPAC military exercises bomb sacred island of Kaho'olawe contrary to wishes of indigenous peoples.

Marshall Islands

Islanders moved from their homelands to make way for 66 nuclear bomb tests, 1947-1958.
Six islands completely evaporated.
March 1, 1954, first H-bomb dropped on Bikini.
The wind direction caused fallout on nearby Rongelap.
Radiation illnesses, cancers, and deformities have developed.

Mururoa

French still testing nuclear weapons on Mururoa Atoll.
Around Tahiti, miscarriages are frequent due to radiactivity, and marine life is dangerous to eat.
Atmospheric tests (41 in all) stopped in 1974. Over 70 underground tests since. Independence leaders are imprisoned.

Kanak struggles for independence from French colonization. Call for independence has increased French military, including building of a base for nuclear-capable subs.

Protected Species

All over the world, people and organizations are working hard to protect animals and plants from disappearing from the earth.

There are about 5 to 10 million species of living things. Most of them are insects. The next most abundant form is plants. Animals other than insects are the smallest group. For each plant species endangered, a number of animal species are endangered.

The forests and wetlands of the world are being destroyed. This means the destruction of many species of plants. After those plants will go the animals that depend on them for food. And after them will go the animals that eat the plant eaters

It used to be said that we were losing one species every year. Now it is said to be one every day. By the end of the century it could be thousands of species every year.

The Past

Apart from insects, at least 80 percent of the animals that became extinct between the year 1600 and the middle of this century were island species. Most of those species were birds.

In that time Hawaii lost twice as many species as North America. This is because an animal living on an island is likely to be adapted to a particular habitat. These plants and animals have evolved in isolation on small islands. When more vigorous plants and animals are introduced, the island organisms die out because they cannot compete. Also, the number of any particular species on an island will be fewer, and a single disaster can wipe out the whole population. Islands therefore need special protection.

Most of the islands of the Pacific are either volcanic or coral islands. In both cases, this means that one day they rose out of the sea, with neither plants nor animals living on them. The seeds of plants came floating along and birds came flying in. Insects arrived, carried on the winds or on the seeds or with birds, but very few land animals came. A bird or a rat can hitch a lift on a boat, but a bear or a kangaroo is less likely to be a successful stowaway. This is why most Pacific island animal species are birds and insects. It is also why most *extinct* Pacific island species are birds and insects.

When people think about animals that are disappearing from the world, they often get very upset about hunting. This is easy to do because hunting can be cruel, but there are two other more important reasons for the extinction of animals.

One is the fact that they have nowhere to live and nothing to eat, because the forests or other places where they live, their habitats, have been destroyed.

The other reason is that different plants or animals have been brought in from elsewhere. These exotic species may compete with the native species and win. They compete for a place to live and for food. The effect is the same as that of habitat destruction. The native plant or animal simply dies and the entire species may eventually die out. Exotic species may also kill off the native species by eating their eggs or their babies or by hunting the adults. The Pacific is full of such stories.

The sparrow and the rat are two of the most familiar and destructive of the introduced species. The sparrow was brought to the Pacific just because city people from Europe liked to see it around, and yet, simply by being there and eating foods that other birds depend on, it has starved or is starving some of the beautiful birds of the Pacific.

The rat came accidentally, in the holds of ships. It brought disease that killed millions of human beings. It competed for food with many small mammals and ate their eggs or their babies. In the process, it helped wipe them out as well. Cats, rats, goats, pigs, deer, rabbits, and many other animals are destroying the habitats of plants, birds, and reptiles in the islands of the Pacific.

Exotic plants where they do not belong: top, prickly pear; bottom, exotic aloes and mother-of-millions growing with native casuarinas and grasses. Australia.

Mangrove plants and animals at risk

Thailand
leaf monkey
orchid 2
lady slipper

Singapore
orchid 9

Taiwan
mangrove 2

Malaysia
crocodile 4
heron 2
bittern 2
egret 2
stork 2
cormorant 1
flying fox 1
macaque 1
orchid 9
mangrove 1

Indonesia
stork 1
Sumatran tiger 1
orchid 1

Australia
Australian
saltwater
crocodile

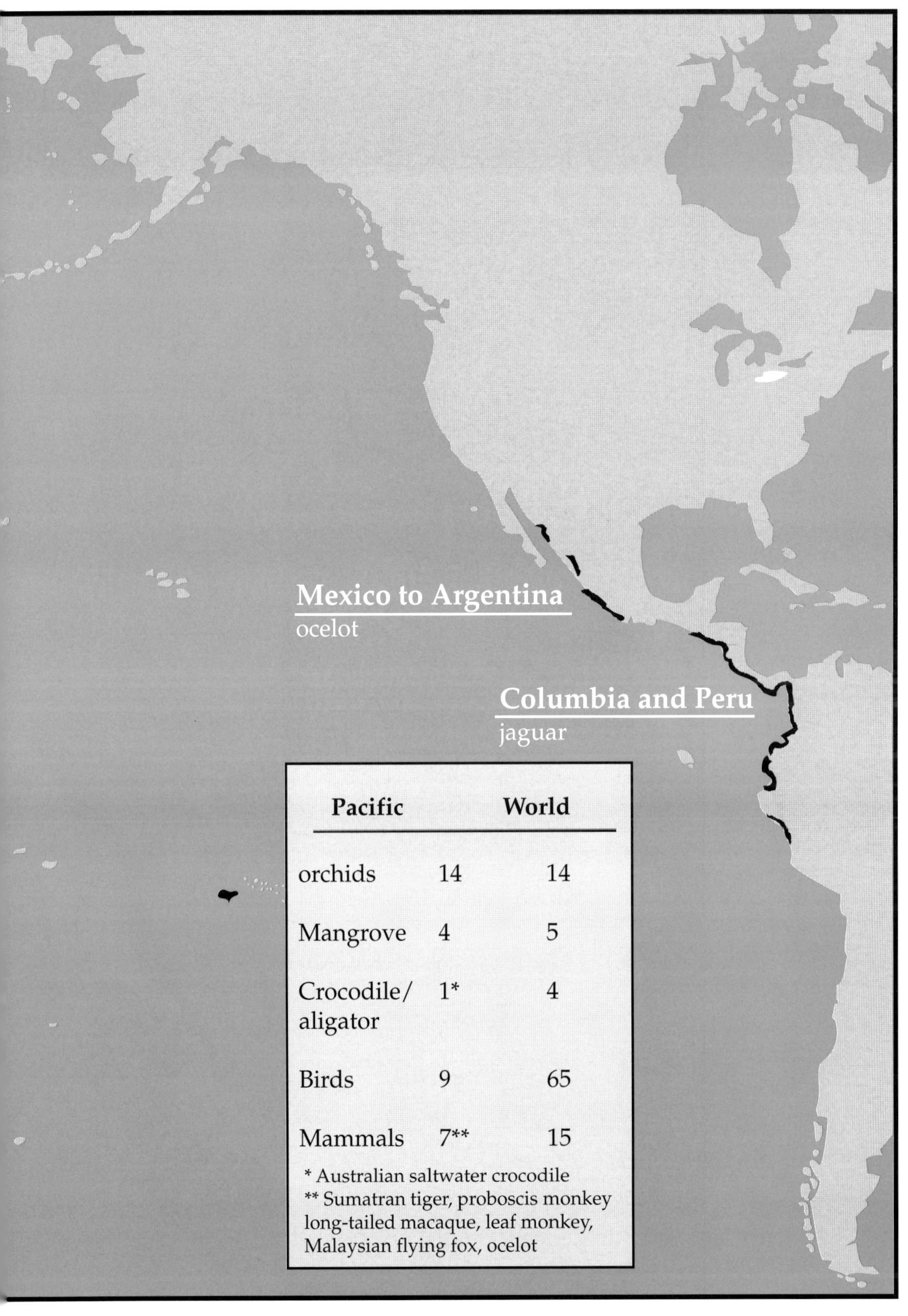

Pacific	World
orchids	14	14
Mangrove	4	5
Crocodile/ aligator	1*	4
Birds	9	65
Mammals	7**	15

* Australian saltwater crocodile
** Sumatran tiger, proboscis monkey long-tailed macaque, leaf monkey, Malaysian flying fox, ocelot

Threatened birds of the Pacific. The numbers represent the number of threatened species in each country.

Canada
6
USA
43
Mexico
35
Central America
58
Colombia
69
Ecuador
64
Peru
75
French
Polynesia
20
Chile
18

To preserve animals, we need to preserve their habitats. This means preserving the plant communities in which they live. It also means not bringing exotic plants or animals to places where they don't belong.

The Future

Why should we try to save species from dying out?

First, there is a moral reason. Although we know so little of what there is to understand about the world and the universe, we already have the power to make major changes in them. For the sake of the people and the creatures of the future, we must use this power carefully.

Second, preserving a wide variety of species is a matter of self-defence. The changes we make in the ecosystem are likely to affect us because we are part of it. Therefore we need to be careful. We may not need a particular species now, but we may find in the future that it would have been useful. New medicines, for example, are constantly being developed from unusual plants. We may also find out that a species was important to us, although we did not know it until it died out and things started going wrong without it.

The plants and animals that we use for food came from wild strains. Scientists have developed new types that have greater yields and are more resistant to disease. These strains are in wider and wider use, but what happens if a new disease strikes? Scientists go back to the wild strains to find one that is more resistant to the new disease. They then breed the two together and produce a new strain.

For example, the world wheat crop depends on only a few different types of wheat. If disease strikes, a huge amount of the world's food is in danger. What would happen to the human race if all the wild strains had been destroyed?

Protected areas

What Areas Should Be Protected?

To protect plants and animals, we have to protect large areas of the earth. This means keeping human beings out, as well as keeping out animals and plants that don't belong there.

It is hard to persuade people not to cut down trees or build houses, and it is even harder to persuade them to give up land. But increasingly, nations are acting to preserve wilderness. How do we decide which land to set aside?

Countries should protect

- places where the wild relatives of useful plants and animals live (for example, the wild relatives of the cow or of wheat or rice)

- places where threatened species live

- places where the whole ecosystem is the only one of its type (for example, Antarctica, the Galapagos Islands, the island of Maui in Hawaii)

- places that are particularly good examples of a certain type of ecosystem (for example, the Great Barrier Reef)

How Do We Protect Them?

Different types of ecosystems need different amounts of protection. Generally a large reserve is better than a smaller one. If the reserve is surrounded by unprotected land, where, for example, cattle are grazing, a large area of the reserve will be in danger of being eaten or trampled by the cattle. Only the very center of the reserve will be safe. Therefore the bigger the reserve, the larger the safe area. Also, some animals need to have areas of their own; they keep other animals of the same species out, and within these territories they breed. If the area of the reserve is not large enough, the animals may not be able to breed and will therefore not survive.

Reserves should be sheltered as far as possible from harm, for example from the harm done by tourists. There should be buffer zones where there are special rules about what may and may not be done.

Reserves should have as much variety within them as possible. For example, the giant panda that lives in China depends on bamboo for its food. There needs to be an alternative food source in case all of its usual food should be destroyed. Shrimp do not only need mangrove swamps to breed in; they also need a path to the open sea.

The Pacific has 40 percent of the protected area of the world. Thirty percent of this area is located in just three countries—the United States (65 million hectares), Australia (35 million), and Canada (23 million).

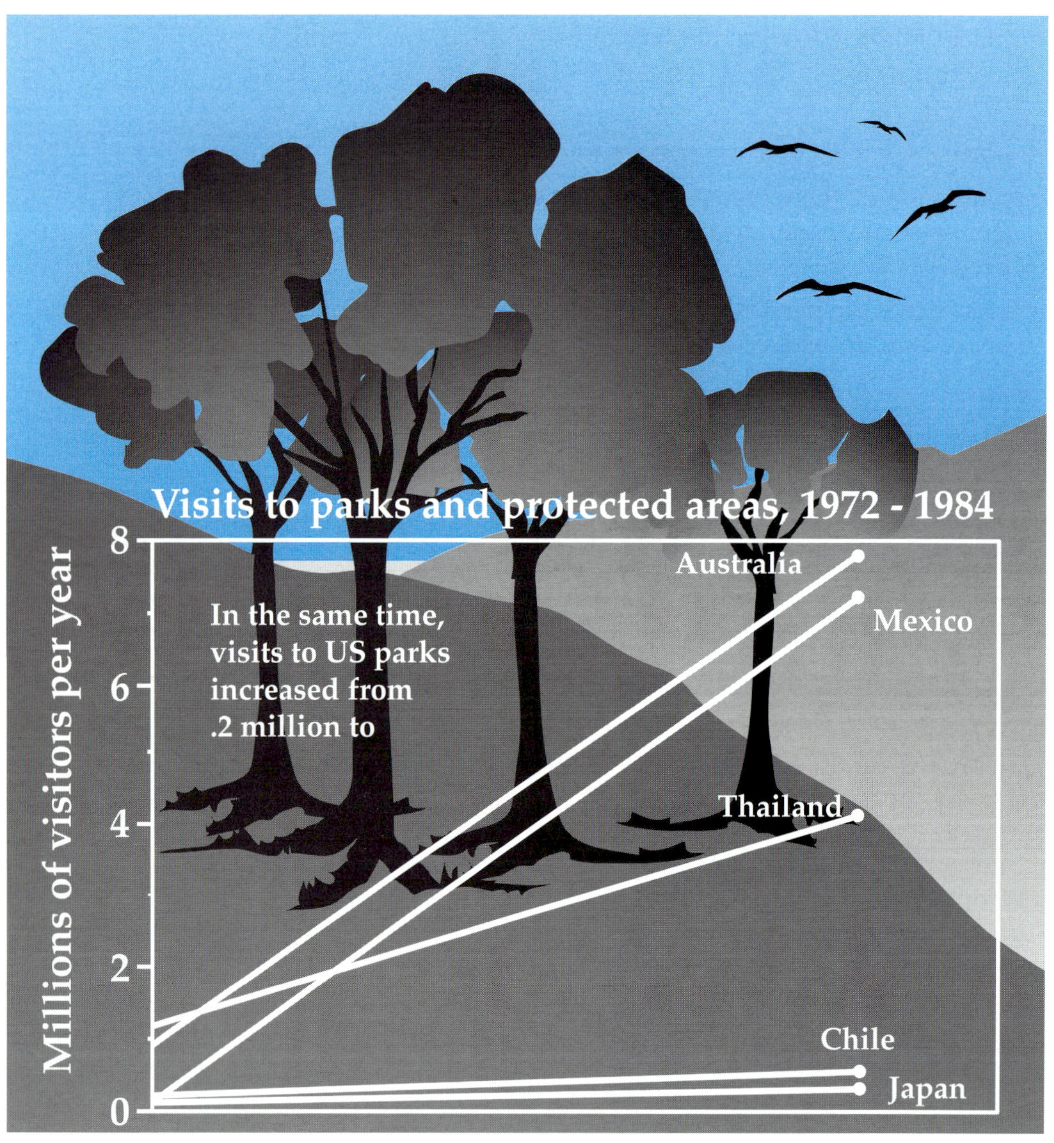

Apart from these three, and a few other countries, the Pacific has a poorly developed system of national parks and protected areas. This is in spite of the fact that many plant and animal species are at risk. Outside of Hawaii, only 50 islands have any parks or protected zones, and half of them are uninhabited islands.

What can we do?

What Is Conservation?

Conservation is one of the major issues of the twentieth century. Until the 1970s many people had never heard of conservation. The resources of the world seemed limitless. When people began to realize how severely those reserves had been exploited and mismanaged, they began to demand that things be put right. The population explosion of the Third World countries, several oil crises, and the unmistakable evidence of global pollution made it clear that change was necessary.

Conservation is concerned with preservation, maintenance, sustainable use, restoration, and enhancement of the natural environment. It is the management of human use of ecosystems so that they can yield the greatest sustainable benefit to people now and still be healthy for the benefit of future generations. Living resource conservation is specifically concerned with plants, animals, and micro-organisms and with the nonliving elements of the environment on which they depend.

What Are the Aims of Conservation?

The aims of conservation are

- to maintain the processes on which life on earth depends (for example, the recycling of nutrients and the cleaning of water)

- to preserve plant and animal species

- to ensure the sustainable use of plants and animals so that they will be available for future generations

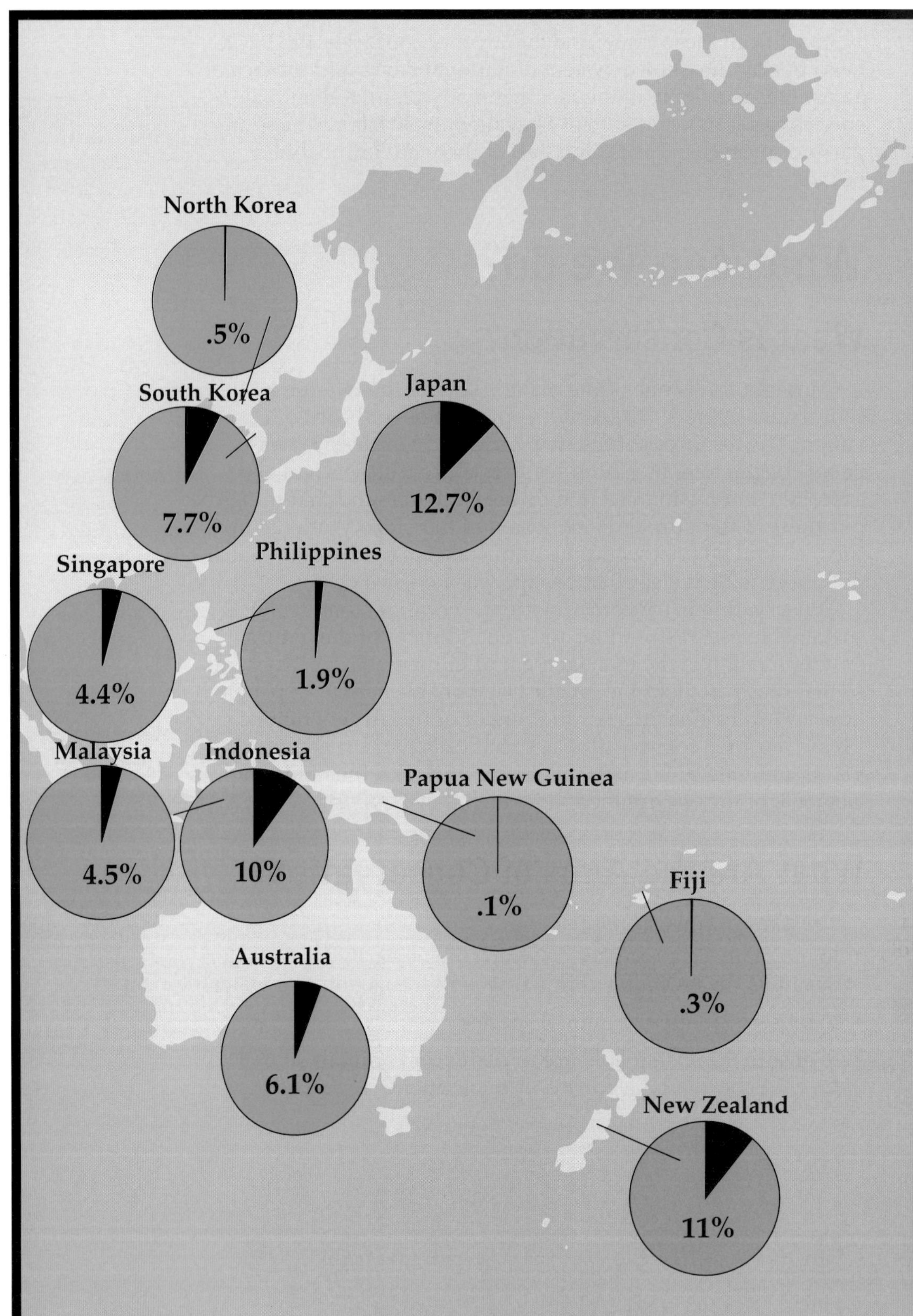

North Korea
.5%
South Korea
7.7%
Japan
12.7%
Singapore
4.4%
Philippines
1.9%
Malaysia
4.5%
Indonesia
10%
Papua New Guinea
.1%
Fiji
.3%
Australia
6.1%
New Zealand
11%

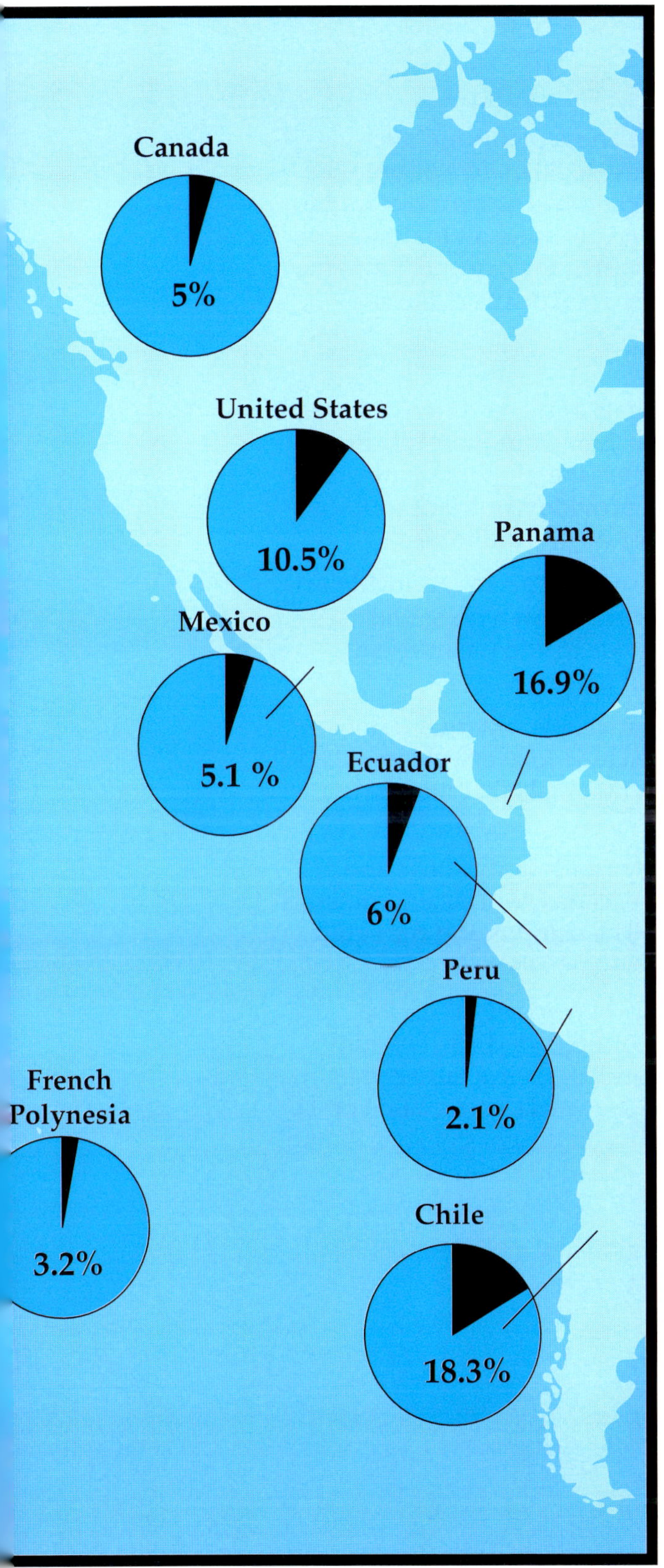

- Because of the increasing population of the world. The more people there are, the greater the pressure on the same amount of land. It has been estimated that about five hectares are needed to support each person.

- Because of improved methods of harvesting. Better boats, equipment, and detection devices have meant that fish tend to be overexploited and habitats destroyed.

- Because of the consumption of nonliving resources. People are rapidly using up new materials such as oil, gas, coal, and minerals. Water is often heavily polluted and the coastal zone is polluted.

- Because of our desire to ensure that the people who come after us do not live in a polluted world and that they do not lack natural resources.

Protected areas in the Pacific. The figure in each circle represents the percentage of that country's total land mass that is nationally "protected" in some way or another.

Glossary

Algae and phytoplankton The water plants. These plants include seaweeds that grow to 30 meters or more in length and one-celled plants that float in the sea. Phytoplankton are so small that they can be seen only through a microscope. From the chemicals of the sea the plants make and become the food that feeds all of the animals of the ocean.

Animal plankton, or zooplankton Microscopic animals of many different types. Some of them can swim, but most just float. The zooplankton eat the phytoplankton, and the two together provide a nutrient soup to support the rest of the life in the sea.

Bacteria Ultramicroscopic organisms found in all parts of the sea. They break down plant and animal parts and waste into the nutrient chemicals to build life anew.

Crustacea Animals with a moveable, external, armor-like shell. They include lobsters, shrimp, and many less familiar animals that may be microscopic.

Mollusks Animals that have rigid, stony shells and a soft body. Oysters, clams, whelks and mussels are all mollusks. The octopus and the squid are mollusks without shells.

Fish Animals with backbones that live in the water. Most are cold-blooded. Fish include sharks and rays and all their relatives that swim among the seaweeds, rocks, and corals. Most ocean fish live in the coastal zone. Some, such as tuna, are found in the open ocean.

Birds Animals with feathers, wings, and warm blood that lay eggs. They include gulls, penguins, and sea eagles.

Mammals	Animals with warm blood that breathe air and feed their young on mother's milk. They include whales, porpoises, seals, bears, dogs, cats, and kangaroos, as well as monkeys and human beings.
Detritus	Broken bits of plants and animals eaten by other animals or decomposed by bacteria. Bone and shell are laid down on the ocean bottom and may some day become limestone rock.
Nutrients	Basic chemicals that must cycle back to build new generations of plants and animals. When a plant or animal dies it is broken down into the chemical nutrients that formed it. Eventually these nutrients are used by other living things and the cycle of life is renewed.
Sediment and rocks	Rock formations shape the shore and ocean bed. Rock breaks into boulders and boulders into gravel, sand, silt, and mud, which cover the seabed and the shore.

Sources and Credits

These sources and credits are listed by chapter, page, and caption.

Introduction

8 *A lighthouse in Oregon.* Jim Larison, Oregon Sea Grant, photograph

10 *An oil rig in Bass Strait . . .* Australian Department of Foreign Affairs and Trade, photograph

12 *The shrinking high seas.* Don Poole, artist. Adapted from *The Times Atlas of the Oceans* (London: Times Books, 1983), pp. 222-223.

14 *High productivity regions . . .* Don Poole, artist. Adapted from *Fish and the Environment: A System* (Honolulu: Curriculum Research and Development Group, 1988), figure 9, p. 19.

Winds and Currents

17 *The Coriolus effect.* Anna Asquith, artist. Adapted from Frederic Martini, *Exploring Tropical Isles and Seas* (Englewood Cliffs, New Jersey: Prentice-Hall, 1984), p. 8.

18 *Routes of the early traders.* Don Poole, artist. Adapted from Christopher Lloyd, *Atlas of Maritime History* (New York: Arco, 1975), pp. 68-69, and David R. MacGregor, *The Tea Clippers: Their History and Development 1833-1875,* 2nd ed. (London: Naval Institute Press, 1983), p. 31.

20 *Effects of a land mass on ocean winds.* Anna Asquith, artist. Adapted from Martini, op. cit., p. 12.

21 **Circulation of the atmosphere.** Anna Asquith, artist. Adapted from Martini, op. cit., p. 6.

21 *Results of the Coriolus effect.* Anna Asquith, artist.

22 *Patterns of surface winds in the Pacific.* Anna Asquith, artist. Adapted from Martini, op. cit., p. 17.

24 *Patterns of surface currents in the Pacific.* Anna Asquith, artist. Adapted from Martini, op. cit., p. 17.

Beaches and Cliffs

26 *Some beaches are formed . . .* Oregon Sea Grant, photograph

27 *A boulder beach . . .* Barry Stranger, photograph

27 *An almost flat beach.* Bob Peisley, Australian Department of Foreign Affairs and Trade, photograph

28 *The gentle slope . . . .* Terry Rowe, Australian Department of Foreign Affairs and Trade, photograph

28 *Violent wave action . . .* John McKinn, Australian Department of Foreign Affairs and Trade, photograph

29 *Different plants . . .* Marguerite Wells, photograph

30 *Plants with long roots . . . Forest and Bird,* photograph

31 *Seaweeds living on rocky shores . . .* Barry Stranger, photograph

32 *Rocky shore—who lives where?* Adapted from *The Beach Book* (Vancouver, B.C.: Western Education Development Group), p. 7, by permission of the publisher. (Address: Pacific Educational Press, Faculty of Education, University of British Columbia, Vancouver, B.C V6 1Z4)

Wetlands and Estuaries

33 *Fine mud and calm water . . .* Barry Stranger, photograph

35 *The wetlands laundry service.* Anna Asquith, artist. Adapted from UNESCO, *Coastal Lagoon Research Present and Future,* Proceedings of a seminar, Duke University Marine Laboratory, Beaufort, North Carolina, August 1978 (Paris: UNESCO, 1981), p. 76.

36 *Salt marshes of the Pacific.* Don Poole, artist. Adapted from Norman Myers, gen. ed., *Gaia: an Atlas of Planet Management* (Garden City, New York: Anchor, 1984), p. 75.

37 *In an estuary . . .* Anna Asquith, artist. Adapted from Russell Sackett, *Edge of the Sea* (Alexandria, Virginia: Time-Life Books, 1983), p. 119.

38 *Strong river, weak tide.* Anna Asquith, artist. Adapted from Russell Sackett, op. cit., p. 103.

40 *Who eats what?* Anna Asquith, artist. Adapted from *Estuary: an Ecosystem and a Resource, Teacher's Manual* (Corvallis, Oregon: Oregon Sea Grant, 1983), pp. 126-127.

42 *Who lives where?* Anna Asquith, artist. Adapted from Thomas M. Niesen, *The Marine Biology Coloring Book* (New York: Barnes and Noble, 1982), chapter 5.

Lagoons

44 *A coastal lagoon . . .* Marguerite Wells, photograph

45 *Different ways . . .* Anna Asquith, artist. UNESCO, *Coastal Lagoon Research Present and Future,* op. cit., p. 63.

46 *Marsh grasses . . .* Marguerite Wells, photograph

46 *Ancient fish pond in Hawaii.* National Park Service, photograph

Mangroves

47 *Some mangroves have prop roots.* Marguerite Wells, photograph

47 *Some have peg roots . . .* Marguerite Wells, photograph

48 *Mangroves help . . .* South Pacific Regional Environment Programme, photograph. Reprinted by permission of SPREP.

49 *In this tide channel . . .* Marguerite Wells, photograph

50 *Mangroves in the Pacific.* Don Poole, artist. Adapted from *Gaia*, op. cit., p. 75, and Peter Saenger, E.J. Hegerl, and J.D.S. Daire, eds., *Global Status of Mangrove Ecosystems* (Gland, Switzerland: International Union for Conservation of Nature and Natural Resources, 1983), pp. 11-12.

52 *A mangrove seed unfolds.* Anna Asquith, artist

53 *Who eats what in a mangrove forest.* Anna Asquith, artist. Adapted from *Global Status of Mangrove Ecosystems,* op. cit., p. 31.

54 *Some products from a mangrove forest.* Don Poole, artist

Coral Reefs and Atolls

55 *There are hundreds . . .* South Pacific Regional Environment Programme, photograph. Reprinted by permission of SPREP.

56 *Cross section of a coral polyp.* Anna Asquith, artist. Adapted from Jon Brodie, ed., *Coral reef ecology* (Suva, Fiji: University of the South Pacific, 1979), p. 10.

57 *A variety of coral types.* Anna Asquith, artist. Adapted from Dietrich H.H. Kühlmann, *Living Coral Reefs* (New York: Arco, 1985), p. 16.

58 *Three basic types of coral reefs.* Anna Asquith, artist. Adapted from Michael King, *Coral Reefs in the South Pacific* (Noumea, New Caledonia: South Pacific Commission, 1988), p. 11.

59 *everyone must be struck . . .* Quotation from Charles Darwin, *The Structure and Distribution of Coral Reefs* (London, 1851; rpt. Berkeley, California: University of California Press, 1976), p. 1. Reprinted by permission of the publisher.

59 *Darwin's sketch of Whitsunday Island . . .* Darwin, op. cit., p. 2. Reprinted by permission of the publisher.

60 *Two views of Bora Bora . . .* Darwin, op. cit., p. 3 and plate 1, figure 5. Reprinted by permission of the publisher.

61 *Formation of an atoll.* Anna Asquith, artist

62 *Distribution of coral in the Pacific.* Don Poole, artist. Adapted from Herold J. Wiens, *Atoll Environment and Ecology* (New Haven: Yale University Press, 1962), p. 230.

Harbors and Cities

64 *Pacific Rim cities with a population over 2 million.* Don Poole, artist. Data from United Nations, *1992 Demographic Yearbook* (New York: United Nations, 1994).

66 *Rural and urban distribution of Pacific Rim cities.* Don Poole, artist. Data from United Nations, *1992 Demographic Yearbook* (New York: United Nations, 1994).

68 *Passenger cars for every 1000 people, 1992.* Don Poole, artist. Data from United Nations Environment Programme, *Environmental Data Report 1993-94* (Oxford: Basil Blackwell, 1993), pp. 326 ff; and "Brunei," Encyclopedia Americana, 1995 ed.

70 *Per capita gross national product around the Pacific, 1992.* Don Poole, artist. Data from *The World Bank Atlas 1994* (Washington, D.C.: World Bank, 1993), pp. 18-19.

72 *Ships cleared to leave port . . .* Don Poole, artist. Data from United Nations, *Statistical Yearbook 1992* (New York: United Nations, 1994), pp. 668 ff.

74 *Rubbish dump . . .* Marguerite Wells, photograph

Pollution

What is Pollution?

74 ff Text based on United Nations Environment Programme, *Cleaning Up the Seas*, UNEP Environment Brief No. 5 (Nairobi, Kenya: UNEP, 1988).

75 *Boom system . . .* Australian Department of Foreign Affairs and Trade, photograph

76 *How the seas are polluted.* Don Poole, artist. Adapted from Essam El-Hinnawi and Manzur H. Hashmi, *The State of the Environment* (London: Butterworths, 1987)

Industrial Pollution

79 *Pollutants in our water.* Don Poole, artist. Data from E. Dejardin, *Illustrated Environmental Studies* (London: Bell and Hyman, 1987), p. 57.

Sewage

81 *Sewage treatment.* Don Poole, artist. Redrawn from figure 10.6 in Dejardin, op. cit. Redrawn by permission of the publisher.

82 *Sign warns of a sewage spill . . .* Marguerite Wells, photograph

82 *Fecal coliforms.* Text based on United Nations Environment Programme, *Safeguarding the World's Water,* UNEP Environment Brief No 6 (Nairobi, Kenya: UNEP, 1988), p. 2.

84 *How clean are our rivers?* Don Poole, artist. Data from United Nations Environment Programme, *Environmental Data Report*, op. cit., p 44-49 and *Environmental Data Report 1993-94*, op. cit., p. 75.

Nuclear Pollution

86 *Nuclear power generated. . .* Don Poole, artist. Data from United Nations, *1986 Energy Statistics Yearbook* (New York: United Nations, 1988).

87 *Proposed methods for dumping . . .* Anna Asquith, artist. Adapted from drawings by Michael Wright, *The Christchurch Press*, 17 Dec. 1988.

88 *Nuclear power stations in the Pacific . . .* Don Poole, artist. Data from United Nations Environment Programme, *Environmental Data Report*, op. cit., p. 253.

90 *The nuclear Pacific, past and present.* Don Poole, artist. Adapted from Stewart Frith, *Nuclear Playground* (Honolulu: University of Hawaii Press, 1987), p. viii, and Gail Russell Chaddock, "France's Finger on Button To Resume Nuclear Testing," *The Christian Science Monitor,* June 13, 195, p. 7. Adapted by permission of the publisher.

92 *Nuclear events affecting the Pacific.* Anna Asquith, artist. Data mainly from Frith, op. cit., p. viii, and Gail Russell Chaddock, "France's Finger on Button To Resume Nuclear Testing," *The Christian Science Monitor,* June 13, 195, p. 7.

94 *The first atom bombs.* Data from the Committee for the Compilation of Materials on Damage Caused by the Atomic Bombs in Hiroshima and Nagasaki, *Hiroshima and Nagasaki: the Physical, Medical, and Social Effects of the*

87): 52. Jacobs' illustration is from Mark F. Meier,"Contribution of Small Glaciers to Global Sea Level," *Science* 226 (1984): 1420.

116 *Southwest Pacific coastline* . . . Don Poole, artist. Adapted from Fergus Clunie and John Gibbons, "Sea Level Changes and Pacific Prehistory," *The Journal of Pacific History* 21 (1986): 64. Adapted by permission of the publisher and Mr. Clunie.

The Ozone Layer

117 *The ozone layer.* Anna Asquith, artist. Adapted from United Nations Environment Programme, *The Changing Atmosphere,* op. cit., p. 6.

118 *Chlorofluorocarbons in the atmosphere.* Don Poole, artist. United Nations Environment Programme, *Environmental Data Report 1993-94,* op. cit., p. 12.

119 *Social effects of damaging the atmosphere.* Anna Asquith, artist. Adapted from United Nations Environment Programme, *The Changing Atmosphere,* op. cit., p. 3.

Coastal Management

121 *The Gold Coast, Australia* . . . Australian Department of Foreign Affairs and Trade, photograph

123 *The sacred sea.* Don Poole, artist. Text adapted from *Between Land and Sea, a Sourcebook for Teachers* (Wellington: Department of Conservation).

Fishing Regulations

124 *Pacific fish catch* . . . Don Poole, artist. Data from *FAO Yearbook. Fishery Statistics. Catches and Landings,* vol. 74 (Rome: FAO, 1994), pp. 101-103, 507-522.

128 *Between 1960 and 1986 the amount of pond-raised fish* . . . Don Poole, artist. Adapted from Han Mukang, Zhao Shusong, and Ge Luiqing, "China's Coastal Environment, Utilization, and Management," *Aquaculture in China* (Chicago: University of Chicago, 1989), p. 233.

Original Peoples

130 *Original peoples of the Pacific* . . . Don Poole, artist. Adapted from Julian Burger, *Report from the Frontier* (London: Zed Books, 1987), p. 10, by permission of the publisher. Data also from United Nations, *1992 Demographic Yearbook* (New York: United Nations, 1994); *1990 Census of Population. General Population Characteristics. United States* (Wash. D.C.: U.S. Department of Commerce, 1992), p. 3; and 1991 Canadian census, cited in Alanna Mitchell, "More Canadians Acknowledge Aboriginal Ancestry," *Globe and Mail.* March 31, 1993, A-1.

134 *When the Pacific became a nuclear testing ground* . . . Don Poole, artist. Adapted from Burger, op. cit., p. 210. Adapted by permission of the publisher.

Protected Species

137 *Exotic plants.* Marguerite Wells, photograph

138 *Mangrove plants and animals at risk.* Don Poole, artist. Data from International Union for Conservation of Nature and Natural Resources, *Global Status of Mangrove Ecosystems,* op. cit., pp. 46-49.

140 *Threatened birds of the Pacific.* Don Poole, artist. Data from United Nations Environment Programme, *Environmental Data Report, 1993-94,* op. cit., pp. 188 ff.

Protected Areas

144 *Visits to parks . . .* Don Poole, artist. Data from United Nations Environment Programme, *Environmental Data Report ,* op. cit., p. 167.

What Can We Do?

146 *Protected areas . . .* Don Poole, artist. Data from United Nations Environment Programme, *Environmental Data Report, 1993-94,* op. cit., pp. 196 ff.

Index

fish ponds, 46, 128
fishing, 19, 20, 34, 75-76, 122, 124-28,
    132
fishing regulations, 126-27, 129
forests, 47, 49, 103, 104, 132, 136, 137
Formosa, 129
France, 83, 92, 93, 94
French Polynesia, 71, 124, 141, 146
freshwater, 34, 38, 39, 44, 47, 79, 96-100
Fujian, 129

Galapagos Islands, 20, 63, 143
Gold Coast, 121
grasses, 30, 38, 40, 45, 46, 102, 119
grazing, 103
Great Barrier Reef, 61, 62, 121, 122, 143
Great Britain, 92, 93, 94, 129, 134
greenhouse effect, 110-16, 119, 120
Greenpeace, 93
gross national product, 70-71
Guadalajara, 65
Guam, 124, 134
Guangzhou (China), 64
guano, 19, 20
Guatemala, 71

habitat, 6, 11, 13, 37, 136, 137, 142, 147
harbors, 34, 64
Hawaii, 10, 45, 46, 63, 82, 99, 102, 129,
    133, 135, 136, 143, 145
Hiroshima, 83, 90, 92, 94
Ho Chi Minh, 64
Hong Kong, 64, 68, 70, 72
Honshu (Japan), 62, 129
humans, impact of, 39, 74-94, 99, 102-
    108, 132, 143
Humboldt current, 20
hydrogen bomb, 92

India, 86
Indian Ocean, 75
Indians, 129, 131, 132
Indonesia, 16, 40, 50-51, 62, 64, 66, 70,
    84, 129, 138, 140, 146
international law, 11
Inuit, 133
iron ore, 27

Japan, 10, 20, 50-51, 62, 64, 66, 68, 70,
    72, 76, 78, 83, 84, 86, 88, 92, 118, 122,
    124, 126, 129, 130, 140, 144, 146
Johnston Island, 63, 91, 92

Kampuchea, 50-51
Kanaky, 134
Kermadec Islands, 63
Kiribati, 96
Korea, 72, 88, 124, 126. *See also* South
    Korea *and* North Korea

lagoons, 11, 33, 44-46, 61, 64, 97
Lima, 65
Line Island, 63
logging, 105, 106
Los Angeles, 65

Malaysia, 50-51, 70, 72, 129, 138, 140,
    146
Malden Island, 91
mangroves, 9, 11, 33, 38, 40, 47-54, 121,
    138, 144
Maoris, 123, 131, 132
Marcus Island. *See* Minami-tori-shima
Mariana Islands, 62. *See also* Northern
    Marianas
marine park, 122
Marlborough Sounds, 105
Marquesas, 20, 63
Marshall Islands, 62, 83, 92, 124, 134
marshes, 33, 34, 36-37, 38, 46
Maui, 143
Melbourne, 64
mercury, 78, 79
Mexico, 51, 65, 69, 71, 73, 88, 122, 125,
    138, 141, 144, 146
Mexico City, 65
Micronesia, 124, 134
Minamata, 78
Minami-tori-shima (Marcus Island),
    10
minerals, 121
mining, 76-77, 103, 132
Monte Bello Islands, 92
Moreton Bay (Australia), 62
Mount Fuji, 129
mud, 33, 38, 39, 40, 44, 47, 48, 49, 105,
    149
Mururoa Atoll, 91, 92, 93, 134

Nagasaki, 83, 90, 92, 94
Nagoya (Japan), 64
Nanjing (China), 64
Nauru, 20
New Caledonia, 51, 62, 66, 116, 124
New Guinea, 116, 140. *See also* Papua
    New Guinea